A BOYS LIFE WITH THE BEAST

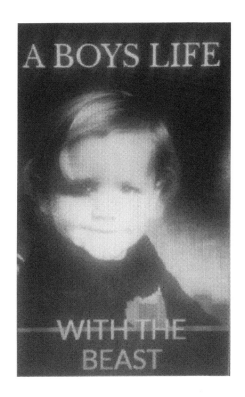

The cries that no one heard

C.S Proctor

Contents

A NOTE FROM THE AUTHOR

I have chosen to tell this true story, which I have written, in my opinion, of my life experience growing up as a child.

Not all parties mentioned in the book want to be known; therefore, all of the names in this book got changed to maintain the dignity, respect, and privacy of the people within it.

INTRODUCTION

My name is Callum, and this is my story.

I have chosen to share something with you, something I found profoundly heart-breaking and challenging to write.

I could never talk with a counsellor about my life or the things that happen to me and was advised to write them down. I have done so in this book and opened up to anyone who wishes to read it.

Do I think it has been worth the pain to write this book? Yes, I do.

Will I ever forgive or forget what happened to me? That depends!

What you are about to read will have detailed information at times and is not for the faint-hearted. I found it deeply disturbing to write and very emotional; however, I felt this was something I had to do.

I do not claim to be a writer, nor am I an educated person. I'm just an average guy, and this book got written from the heart, and as a self-help tool for me personally.

CHAPTER ONE

Age 1 to 4

_____

MEET THE FAMILY

And so, my life begins.

Our first family home is a tiny cramped flat, located within a small run-down council estate. There are significant gangs that gather around the shops and spray-paint the walls with gang symbols. Almost everyone knows each other's business, and most of the people within the estate are collecting benefits.

There is me, my mother, Mary, my father Ronald and my older sister Beth.

Life is not that great living on the estate, and our family has little money, and we are living on government benefits. My mother always makes do with what she has and always does her best to make sure we have a full stomach, with clean clothes on our back; they might not be the latest fashion, but they keep us warm.

I believe in the beginning; my father genuinely cared for my mother and our family. However, his harsh upbringing deeply affected him, and the emotions burning within him moulded him into the beast that he became. He has a chip on his shoulder and often complains about being the black sheep of his family.

My father's father worked on a military base, and he liked old-style cars, he worked hard and also liked the ladies, so much so that he got charged with bigamy. He passed away when my father was still young, and I never got to meet him. Then my Grandmother remarried her second husband, Grandpa Jim. Grandpa Jim was loving and caring to all the family; he also worked on a military base and earned excellent pay. He was very caring and generous to my Grandmother; unfortunately, he too died at a young age. My Grandmother wastes no time meeting her third husband, Arthur. Arthur is years more youthful than my father, and he is a hideous looking man with severe acne that oozed with pus. Arthur is so disgusting and has blond matted shoulder-length hair, even the kids in the neighbourhood called him Freddy Krueger. Arthur also walked with a limp, and he never got accepted into our family. He is a vile man and a child sex offender; we all refer to Arthur as Peg Leg.

My father has two sisters and two brothers, Carol, Jane, Josh and Bobby.

My aunt Carol was born blind, and she moved from Scotland to England at a young age. She is a very loving aunt and went on to marry a successful government official. They purchased a large house together and had several children.

My father's older sister, my aunt Jane is also very caring and loving, she has a hard side to her, and we all know not to step on her toes. Aunt Jane also moved away to England at a young age; she too had several children then purchased a large house and opened a childcare business.

My father's other brother Josh is a tough guy, and he picked on my father at times. My Uncle josh has a thirst for success, and he runs his own business within the building trade, he purchased a beautiful house in the upmarket area of the community. His company becomes very successful, very fast, and he too started his own family.

My father's oldest brother Bobby was evil, and he bullied my father then physically and sexually abused him all through his childhood. Bobby got forced to move out of the community and relocated into the city. The family discovered that Bobby had gone to jail as he had become part of a child sex circle, and got prosecuted. Everyone in the family disowned him after he went to prison, and they never again spoke of him.

I got told my uncle Bobby had died not long after moving to the city; it could be possible he is still alive, and my family want people to think he is dead.

My father never got closure, or a chance to confront my uncle Bobby for the sexual abuse, and it ate away at him. At times my father struggles to control his anger and emotions.

My father is never content with his life, always complaining his family leave him out, and he feels like a failure compared with his brother Josh.

As time passes, my father becomes more jealous of his siblings, more so of my Uncle josh and his success. We live in the same area as Uncle Josh; However, both families are on different sides of the fence. My Uncle josh has purchased a large house in the upmarket area, has a nice car and started a business. Uncle Josh is doing so well with his life, and my father has not done so well, my father has a council house with no job, no car, and is receiving benefits. My father never came right out and said he is envious of his brother; however, his actions make it very clear how he feels. He would get outraged at times or even lash out if you mention anything about the achievements and wealth of his brother Josh.

Our family don't live long in the run-down part of the community, the flat is too small, and every day there is trouble on the streets. My mother hates having to live there, and she makes it clear that she wants to move out.

My mother and father struggle, pulling together and trying to make things work, it's ok in the beginning, and both my parents appear to get through one day at a time.

As time passes, my parents' struggle to get through becomes more evident, and it has become a strain on their relationship; things gradually start to become toxic. My parents are continually arguing and bickering, and it is over small things.

Having their first house together with two kids is proving to be complicated. My parents always had their own independence, and now having to live as a family unit is proving to be a challenge. My father craved a dominant role in the relationship and wanted to be the man of the house. My mother is very outspoken and liked to make her own choices in life; it would appear their fight for leadership has begun.

My father starts subtle arguments with my mother. At first, it is petty things, like not having the dinner ready on time, or making a joke how a woman's place is in the kitchen. The arguments between my parents became daily, and with each conflict, the level of intensity would rise.

One-day things stepped over that line, and my parents got physical with each other, it is equal at first, and both attack each other. After each fight, my father, turns on his charm and says sorry to my mother, and she always forgives him, and they make up; until the next argument, and it will all start over.

My mother suffered from postnatal depression after she gave birth to me. This depression is the start of a long line of mental health problems for my mother, and my father takes advantage of her illness; using it to break her down slowly.

As time passes, the fights between my parents, become more and more aggressive, not just verbally but physically. My poor mother is no match for him, especially in her mental state.

During one of the physical fights between my parents, my father manages to overpower my mother completely, he drags her into the bathroom and smashes her face off the sink. My father only stops when he noticed all the blood going everywhere. He hit my mother's face so hard on the bathroom sink it broke, along with her nose.

One time, he smashed up the flat, wrecking all of the furniture and breaking all of the windows. I was just a baby at this time, and I am sleeping under the window on the sofa, as my father smashed the window all of the glass shards fell onto the couch, covering me in the glass. My poor mother tried her best to fight back; however, my father is just too strong and always won in the end, with each fight, he is gradually grinding her down.

One night, three men turn up at the flat door, they have gained access to the outer door of the property and claimed to be looking for someone. All three of the men had knives with them, and as the men tried to gain access to the house, my mother, seeing the blades cried out. My parents managed to slam the door closed, preventing the men from getting into the house. However, the three men don't leave the close; they stand there taking turns at kicking and banging on the door trying to gain access.

The police got called, and as they arrived at the scene, the three men made a run for it. However, one of the men got arrested, and the police later discovered it is a case of mistaken identity. The three men had come to the wrong address.

The whole experience pushes my mother over the edge, and she uses the three men coming to our door as ammunition to force the council to rehouse our family. Soon after the incident, the local council offer our family a new home in a nice neighbourhood. This house is perfect for my parents as it has everything, including a school on the doorstep.

This house move will be the fresh start needed for our family.

CHAPTER TWO

Age 4 to 6

_____

NEW HOUSE & *PEG LEG*

The new house is a spacious five apartment, and it is massive in comparison to the small cramped flat in which we were living. The front of the house has a decent-sized garden that looks onto a play maze, and just beyond is an underpass that opens out onto a vast play park. The park has everything a kid would need, a full-size football field, swings, climbing frames, and lots of trees for climbing on. The back of the house has a small garden that looks on to our school, from my bedroom window on the top floor, you can see for miles, it feels like I am at the top of the world. Inside the house is just as impressive, I walked in, and I'm amazed by it, the house has five floors, and every level has rooms on them, it's incredible.

Floor one. Kitchen, dining area, bedroom, and storage cupboard.

Floor two. Laundry room.

Floor three. Sitting room and bedroom.

Floor four. Landing.

Floor five. Bathroom, bedroom and a large storage room that could become a spare room.

The new house is very spacious, and we all love it, and even the neighbours appeared to be friendly and welcoming to our family. It is like a new lease of life for us, and everyone is smiling, my father even seems to be happy.

My mother has also just discovered she is pregnant, and now

everything seemed to be on the up, a new house and a fresh start.

Most of our relatives live within the immediate vicinity, and my parents liked this as a babysitter is available at short notice.

My Grandmother on my father's side also stayed a short walk away, and she lived with her new toy-boy, Peg Leg.

My Papa Mack, my mother's father, his house is on the far side of the park, opposite ours. Papa Mack is an alcoholic, and he has a quick temper.

My Papa Mack and my Nana Rose have separated, as he never treated her right, and his drinking drove her away, they both got a divorce and chose not to talk to each other.

My Great Grandpa Ward on my father's side stayed a few hundred yards away. He would babysit us at times to allow my parents some quality time together, and to work on a better relationship. Grandpa Ward is in his nineties and smelled like old furniture, he smoked a pipe and has a combover hairstyle; he is a lovely wee man, the perfect Great Grandpa.

When Grandpa Ward is babysitting my sister and me, we always tell each other ghost stories and get ourselves so terrified. His combover and his armchair cast a shadow on the wall it appeared to look like a monster with horns and a distorted body. My mother points toward the shadow and says if you two don't behave for your old Grandpa Ward, That's Old Nick the Devil on that wall, and he will come for you. My sister and I spend hours just staring at his shadow on the wall and frightening each other every time it moved.

My Grandmother's house is very different from Grandpa Wards; it is a large house with an extension and conservatory, and all the grandkids would meet up at her place. The house has loads of teddies, fruit machines, all the latest gadgets, soda stream machine and always loads of cakes, biscuits, and chocolate sweets; I think Peg Leg makes it that way for a purpose.

My grandmothers garden is large, she has a dog called Glen, and the house always smells of freshly baked cakes. All the things kids love is at my Grandmother's house; what kid wouldn't like going to granny's house with all those goodies and a pet dog.

My Grandmother was in a bus crash, and she took the bus company to court and sued them, receiving a generous settlement. After the bus accident, my Grandmother became less active and eventually became morbidly obese and struggled to get around. Peg Leg encourages my Grandmother to purchase a mobility scooter, which he loves to use himself. Over time Peg Leg will use this scooter to take advantage of children and aid him for his sick pleasures.

Peg Leg is a very creepy man; he sits on the large chair and has Glen my Grandmother's dog sit on his lap, then he fondles the dog and does strange things to it. One day my aunts seen him, she asked him what are you doing to that poor dog? Peg Leg stopped fondling the dog and started laughing, then he said awe, but my wee Glen likes it when I do it. My aunt just shook her head with disgust then walked out of the room.

Later that day, my aunt spoke with my Grandmother regarding him touching up the dog. However, when anyone says anything against Peg Leg, my Grandmother always defends him. She says to my aunt, he is good to me, and my family are not here twenty-four seven to look after me, just leave him alone, he is the only one here for me when you lot go home.

One day I am in my Grandmother's house alone with Peg Leg, he is in the kitchen, and I am on the landing playing with my toy cars. I can hear Peg Leg moving around, and the clinking of his belt buckle. I have this eerie feeling come over me, and I know something isn't right. I then see him walk from the kitchen into the hall, and I continue to sit at the top of the stairs playing with my toy cars. I don't give him any attention or look at him; however, I can feel his presence and know he is staring at me, so I turn my head and look at him. What I see is Peg Leg standing there with his belt unclipped, his zip open and he is fully exposed, he is glaring right at me and masturbating himself. Peg Leg never utters a word he just stands there staring directly at me. Even when I looked right at him, he just continued. With shock, fear and panic, I jump to my feet and run out the front door, and I don't look back, I just run as fast as I can, until I'm home.

When I arrive home, I run into the Living room and give my mother the biggest hug ever and start sobbing. I am crying so much, and she keeps wiping my tears away and asking me to stop crying, saying she can't understand me under all those tears. Then she says tell mum what's wrong, what has happened; eventually, I calm down and start to talk. I say to her Peg Leg showed me his little man. My mum looks at me and asks, what do you mean his wee man? I reply to her, his Winkey mum his Winkey; He was playing with it in front of me.

My mother's friend Avon is in the house, and she sits me down in between herself and my mother on the sofa and says very calmly and softly. Callum son, you must tell us exactly what you have seen? I then explain in detail what happened and how he made me feel scared and uncomfortable. My mother and Avon spend the rest of the day whispering to each other about things and reassuring me that everything is ok.

When my father arrives home that night, I can hear my mother telling him what has happened. Before long things turn into an argument and both are shouting at each other. My mother is telling my father, she is not happy, she wants something done about it, and her kids will not be going back to my Grandmother's house. I then hear the front door bang shut, it's my father leaving, and I'm sure he is going to my grandmothers, and I'm worried about what he is going to do.

The next day I find out my father has confronted Peg Leg, and when he confronted him, Peg Leg just stuttered at my father saying that he had forgotten I was in the house. He said it was merely all just a big misunderstanding and kept apologising for his actions. My father decided to beat Peg Leg up for what he had done, then told Peg Leg to be more careful in the future.

About one week later, My Grandmother comes to our house in her little scooter, and she talks to my parents regarding what had happened.

After my Grandmother leaves, I can hear my mother and father, arguing downstairs. I am not sure what my Grandmother has said to my parents; however, they were all back on talking terms with my Grandmother, and all appears forgiven. I get the impression my mother did not agree; however, she fears my father, and he manipulated her to talk to my Grandmother.

A few days passed, and I am sent back over to my Grandmother's house, she is babysitting my sister and me. I feel like every-one except myself has forgotten about what Peg Leg did. I am troubled inside and very nervous around Peg Leg, and he just keeps glaring at me.

I do not want to be there and feel very confused as to why my father made me go back, especially with Peg Leg in that house. I have so many thoughts running through my mind; did my par-ents not believe me. Perhaps they thought I have told a lie or ex-aggerated what has happened, do they deem what he did to me ok? I am afraid of my father, so I don't say anything, I know how angry my dad can get when questioned.

I have no choice but to continue going to my grandmothers, and when I'm there, Peg Leg starts to behave differently around me. He is singling me out from any activities, by saying there is no room in the car for me. He takes my cousins, and my sister to the shop for sweets and they all go for drives, I get told to stay at home with my Grandmother. I know Peg Leg is punishing me for talking out against him.

After the incident with Peg Leg at my grandmothers, my

mother and father are arguing all the time. My mother makes it clear; she is not happy at the decision for her kids to return to my Grandmother's house, especially with Peg Leg being there. My father has such control over my mother at this point, and even though she disagreed, my mother gives in to keep the peace. There is only so far that my mother can push my father before he erupts, and the house gets smashed.

My mother's father, Papa Mack, would come up to our new house and visit, and on several occasions, Papa Mack has been blind drunk. Looking from our window, we could see Papa Mack staggering up through the park, coming from the pub at closing time. As Papa Mack reached the underpass, my mother tells us, right kids, switch off all the lights and pretend we have all gone out, let's see who can keep quiet for the longest. My mother makes us all sit in the dark, very still and in complete silence, hoping he will leave. Papa Mack is standing chapping at the door, swaying back and forth for a long time, then started to shout through the letterbox, I know you are in their Mary, now answer the door to your old dad. If we were lucky, he would eventually leave.

On the occasions that Papa Mack did manage to enter the house, he runs my father into the ground, telling my father how much of a no-good bum and waste of space he is. When my father and Papa Mack argue it gets very heated and at times physical.

Any time Papa Mack got into the house drunk and then finally left, it always resulted in my father verbally abusing my mother. I love my Papa Mack for being so nasty to my father, and my father deserved every bit of it. However, it has its downside, my father gets mad, and the house always gets smashed up in an argument after Papa Mack has left.

Nana Rose rarely visited the new house, and she said its due to my father abusing the kids, and the way he speaks to my mother. She tells my father it's not acceptable, and she won't sit and watch that happen. Nana Rose hates my father, and she does not try to hide how she feels toward him.

My father is always so cruel to my mother and continually calling her names. He will say to her, look at you, you're a fat ugly bitch, you make me sick, and I don't know what I saw in you, your nothing but a fat bastard. He continually insults her, keeping her with low self-esteem, and she is slowly losing all her confidence. Even now, with my mother being heavily pregnant, my father never lets up on her; he is relentless. Every day there is a multitude of insults, sometimes she won't even answer him back, she just puts her head down and cleans up the mess he makes.

My poor mother is always trying to do her best to please everyone. She runs around all day hand and foot after my father, she makes him tea, and he bounces it off the wall and shouts at her, that's not tea its piss water, then has her clean up the mess he made.

My mother makes his dinner, and he throws it across the room, then shouts at her, it's fucking rotten are you trying to poison me, do you think I'm stupid or something? He is always complaining his dinner is too cold, or it's not cooked right. He calls her a lazy fat bitch, telling her that everyone else's wives can cook, and then says to her what the fuck happened to you?

My father continues every day grinding my mother down, pushing her to breaking point; he is so cruel and heartless to her.

Then my mother decides she's had enough, they have this explosive fight, and this time my mother fights back. She completely loses her cool and is like a woman possessed; even her voice changes.

I know things are going to explode, as both of them start to shout at each other, it gets louder and louder, and I got trapped in the kitchen between them. I want to get out, but I'm too scared to pass my father standing in the doorway, so I just run and hide in the corner of the kitchen behind the laundry basket.

My mother starts to smash everything in the kitchen, picking up the plates from the table and throwing them at my father, then she throws the dishes on the sink and the rack at him. She is screaming at him. My father's face is a picture; for a second, he looks scared of her. She then grabs the pot of soup on the cooker and throws it; the soup goes across the room and up the walls. Even the dining table gets upturned, the kitchen is utterly wrecked, and everything is everywhere. My father is standing in the doorway the whole time, as my mother is going crazy, he just watches her every move.

I'm not sure if my mother has reacted this way because she is hormonal with her being pregnant, or if she finally has taken enough of his crap and just snapped.

My mother begins to calm down and stops throwing things around, then she just sits in the middle of the kitchen and starts to sob. My father looks her up and down, smirked and says, well now that you finished, you're going to have to clean it, and walks out the kitchen and up the stairs.

My father spent that evening upstairs watching tv and playing on his computer. My poor mother spent the evening downstairs crying in the kitchen and cleaning up all the mess.

About a week passes, the atmosphere in the house is tense, and my parents have not spoken a word to each other, and another argument erupted. Both my parents are standing on the top landing, and my father decides to teach my mother a lesson. This time he never just stood there staring at her, he hits her a few times then he grabs her by the hair and starts to drag her along the hallway. My mother is screaming at him; please don't, please don't hit me, I'm fucking pregnant. He doesn't care and pulls her by her hair, he pulls her down all the stairs one by one, all five floors until they reached the bottom, my mother is screaming and begging for him to stop. My mother is nearing the end of her pregnancy, and my father drags her down the stairs. He is shouting at her, you are nothing but a slut, a cow, and that fucking thing inside you is not mine, I'm going to rip it right fucking out of you. He then starts to accuse my mother of sleeping with his brother and friends; he is acting like a crazed mad man; he puts his hands around her throat and starts to strangle her. My mother is just lying there with her face going purple, and he only stops when my sister and I start trying to pull him from her, we are screaming and pleading with him to leave her alone.

Immediately after assaulting her, my father starts to apologise, saying he is sorry, and it is because she drove him to do it. If she hadn't wrecked the kitchen the other day, then ignored him, none of this mess would have happened.

My mother stands up, wipes her tears from her face, she then dresses my sister and me, and takes us out of the house to get away from him; she tells him she just wants some breathing space.

The weather is terrible outside, and the rain and hail are bouncing off the ground, the wind is gale force, it's horrendous. She walks us around for hours and hours; the pain in my ears with earache is excruciating. So, I start crying and asking her if I can go home. My mother has this detachable hood on her jacket; she unclips the hood and places it on my head, I ask her again can we go home, and she just keeps repeating herself. We can't go back, I know you want to, but I am sorry for this; I will make this better, I am so sorry, we can't go back.

After some time and walking for miles, around in circles and my mother ranting to herself, she finally decides to return home. As soon as we return, she makes us get stripped out of our wet clothes and sent us upstairs to watch tv. She tells us not to come down; she has to talk to our father.

The next morning when I wake, my mother is in the kitchen she is acting as usual and behaving like yesterday never happened. She makes everyone breakfast, then sends us off to school, and cleans the house.

That night when we return from school, she makes everyone dinner, then after doing my homework sends us to bed.

I think this is when my father has finally beat my mother into submission, and her life with him is no longer a marriage. She has become subservient to him, and he makes sure she knows it.

My mother soon gave birth to my younger brother Steve, and after he is born, she is struggling to cope. My father is providing little if any assistance, and it is evident my mother is on the verge of a breakdown.

My parents have no money; both are chain smokers and are on the lowest benefits; things have got tough. We can't afford new clothes, and my sister and I both ware hand me down clothes from our cousins. My parents start to borrow more money to pay off the debt collectors, and they will borrow from anyone who will give them some cash, Provident, Shop check, Black Horse, the list is endless.

My mother does everything, cooks and cleans, gets us up and out for school, runs after my father hand and foot and is looking after my baby brother. She has no support from my father, and he would much rather play his computer all day, things are just getting way too much for her.

I hate my father for how he treats my mother, and my sister shares my feelings toward him. He is so evil and cruel, and we both wish him dead.

Even the neighbours can see our family is struggling, sometimes our neighbour Glenda comes to the door to hand in food; she makes the best shepherd's pie. Glenda always makes some excuse; she would say I had the family around, and I just made far too much, so I hope you don't mind me handing it in, I would hate to see it go to waste. Being polite, my mother just said thank you and accept the food; however, my father put it into the bin when he knew it came from Glenda. He tells my mother, you don't know what that old cow has done to it, I'm not eating that shit, she's probably taken a piss in it.

My Uncle Josh, who is in the construction business, offers my father a job. The job is on the side for some extra cash to help our family out. My father jumps at the chance, and once again, things seem to be getting back on track. My father starts to treat my mother with a bit of care and respect, and my mother's mental health appears to be improving. With my father out working for most of the day, everyone has the space to breathe and relax. My mother even seems to get some of her old confidence back, she becomes friends with the neighbours, and they would pop in for a cup of tea and a chat when my father is at work. It is pleasant to see my mother being happy again, and the house being a bit more relaxed.

When my father realises, my mother has friends in the house when he is out at work, he becomes angry. He starts making all sorts of accusations, accusing my mother of sleeping around with everyone. He began to shout at her; you think I am stupid while I'm out working, you are in here fucking every tom dick and harry. My father has become even more controlling and green-eyed than before, telling her that our house is like a pigsty, and she can't have anyone in. It is like my father is trying to isolate her and wants her to have no self-control.

After a time, the construction business got quiet, and my father is back at home full time. With no job or extra cash coming into the house, my father has time to burn. He becomes worse than ever, grinding my mother back down until she becomes even lower than before.

Then one day, my mother tries to impress him and make an effort, she dresses herself up and puts makeup on. My father is horrible to her, and he starts saying, your face is too fat for makeup, there's no point putting it on, it's just too ugly. Who would want to look at that fat ugly face, and now you look like a fat repulsive clown, why don't you do us all a favour and just scrub it off? My mother is devastated with his constant insults, and it doesn't take long before she stops caring about herself. She stops wearing her makeup and makes no effort what so ever to wear decent clothes. My father has stripped her of her confidence and her self-esteem once again.

Things slowly start to get worse, and my father is not only verbally abusive toward my sister and me, but he also becomes physically abusive. He makes us follow strict rules in the house, and everything must be in its place, or we will get punished.

The first time he punishes me is for looking at him the wrong way; he asked me to pick something up and put it back, I turn and look at him, and I possibly made a face without thinking. So, he slaps me on my head, knocking me across the room. It is so painful, and I start to cry, he shouts in my face, I hardly fucking touched you, but if you are going to cry, I will give you a reason to be fucking crying. He then takes off his belt and starts whipping me full force across my back. I'm screeching and dancing around in pain; I have never felt pain like this. My father just grabs me looks me in the face and shouts, now you can fucking cry, get to your room. The belt didn't half sting, and it leaves me with marks across my back and has broken my skin.

After that day, I yell and scream anytime he hits me with his belt, I try my hardest not to cry, but it is just so painful. He would grab me by the scruff and yell into my face, stop that fucking crying, or you will get it again, the belt makes me terrified of him, and I instantly jump if he asks me to do anything.

My mother starts to notice that my new-born brother Steve, never flinched to any loud noises or with my father shouting all the time. He mostly just sleeps through their arguments, so my mother becomes concerned something is wrong with his hearing. Then one day at school, my mother is standing directly under the school bell, as the bell rang everyone jumped. However, my baby brother continued to sleep, so to be sure it is not a coincidence, several people standing their shout and clap their hands. They do it right by my brother's head, and once again, my brother never flinched with all the noise they made, he just continued to sleep.

After what happened in the school, my mother took my brother Steve to the doctors for a check-up. The doctors discover my brother has a problem with his bone structure and requested more tests. They say that the soft spot on top of my brother's head appears to have swelling, and he will need to go into hospital for a major operation.

After several life-threatening operations with lengthy periods in the Children's Hospital, the doctors inform the family, my brother Steve is deaf. There is nothing they can do to change this, and he will be unable to hear or speak for the rest of his life. The doctors then discovered that my brother also has a degenerative eye condition, and it will eventually render him completely blind. My poor brother Steve one day, will not only live in a world of complete silence but a world of nothing but darkness.

The whole family gets involved in being able to communicate with my brother, and our family got given little booklets to learn basic sign language. Then My mother arranges for our family to go to classes and learn sign language correctly. It is a sad time for our family, yet also exciting to be taught an entirely new language. My sister and I sign to each other all the time, it is fantastic that no one can understand us, it is like our very own secret language.

My brother Steve never has the same fear for my father as we do, with him having no hearing, he never hears the verbal attacks and smashing of things in the house.

My sister and I do not want to go to my Grandmother's house because of Peg Leg. however, we have to go as my Grandmother babysits our cousins and us. On occasion, Peg Legs nieces would also be there, and we all play at my Grandmothers together. We all played with cards, toys and do arts and crafts, and one time we even built a mini fort in the back garden.

On this day, we are all playing hide and seek. It is a miserable day outside, so we all just played within the house.

During our game of hiding and seek, I had found everyone other than my little cousin. I then heard his voice in the bathroom; however, my cousin is not the only voice I hear in the bathroom; I can also overhear Peg Leg whispering. I can't make out what is said; however, I start making lots of noise outside the bathroom door. At the time, I did not think anything sinister is happening, and I start shouting that's cheating, you can't lock yourself in the bathroom.

My mother shouts from the downstairs kitchen your dinner is ready kids, come and get it, none of us goes downstairs as my cousin is still in the bathroom, he won't unlock the door and come out. My mother shouts up the stairs for a second time; I said dinner. I think my mother realise something is not quite right and screams right kids what's going on up there? I told you dinners are ready. I yelled back to my mother; he is cheating; he has locked the door, and he won't come out. Just at that point, my mother came into visual range at the foot of the stairs. The bathroom door slowly opens, and my poor cousin comes running out, his face is scarlet red, and he is sweating profusely, then Peg Leg walks out of the bathroom at the back of him.

My mother looks directly at Peg Leg, and you can tell she is angry by her face, and then she said in a sharp, angry tone,

What the fuck has been going on in there? Peg Leg replied with a stuttering voice nothing; nothing has been going on Mary; he just came in there to hide. My mother walks over to my cousin, crouches down in front of him and asks? Are you all right son, my cousin replies to my mother in a timid shallow voice, yes, Aunt Mary, I'm ok, I am only hiding, my cousin's face is still scarlet red. Peg Leg then looks directly at my cousin and says, see he is playing, just like I said all along.

Many years later and due to a court error, we sadly discover that Peg Leg had taken my cousin into the bathroom and raped him. Over the coming years, we will find that Peg Leg has committed many more acts of indecency to children.

CHAPTER THREE
Age 6 to 9

MEETING KAREN
& *FATHERS RULES*

The first friend I see when I move into the new house is Karen. Karen is something else, she has a temper like a volcano, and when she lets it go, everyone knows about it. Karen lives with Glenda, the local busybody, Glenda goes to church every Sunday, runs the tuck shop at the school and is in the local neighbourhood watch. She is also a foster carer and has a multitude of different children pass through her home. Glenda initially fostered Karen; however, later adopts her into the family.

On the first day, I meet Karen; I mind my own business as I play on the maze wall across from our new house. The wall I'm standing on is about 4ft on one side and 6ft on the other, I have no friends, and for the first time, I see Karen.

I start walking along the wall of the maze, as Karen is approaching. Karen has an innocent look; freckles dotted over her cute little nose, bright emerald green eyes, and long brown hair in two pleats, small red ribbons, and a knitted red cardigan.

I say hi, I'm Callum I've just moved into the street. She responded saying, I'm Karen, and I'm the best fighter here, and she began to walk along the pavement beside the wall. Before I could blink Karen has grabbed my ankles and yanked my feet out from under me. My ribs are the first thing to hit the wall, and it knocks the wind out of me, as I fall over the wall, I ran my side down the rough edge and land flat on my stomach. However, the very innocent little Karen continues, she jumps over the wall and sits on my back, she pulls at my hair, yanking my head back and then sinks her teeth into my head. Karen then jumps up and runs off like the wind and disappears into one of the houses.

Laid out on the ground with no idea as to what has just happened, I start to get my breath back, as I stand up to check myself over. I have grazed my ribs, have a bleeding head, and also grazed my knee.

I limp back to my house, and I notice my jumper has torn down one side, it must have caught on the wall as I had fallen; I know my father will be furious at me.

As I walk into my house crying, I am afraid and not sure if it's because of the shock of what just happened, or the fear of my father when he sees my jumper.

To my surprise, my father does not care about my jumper or the fact I am injured; He goes into a complete rage when he realises it is a girl that has beaten me up.

My father demands I went back outside and beat up Karen; he is so angry for what she has done. I started to cry and refused; this just infuriates my father even more, and he decides to beat me up for not going back outside. The duration of that day is difficult, as my father continually calls me a coward, a wimp and a little sissy. He also tells me I've gotten myself grounded for the rest of the day, and I should get out of his sight and stay in my room.

About an hour has passed, and my father spots Karen from the window, he shouts me back into the living room and asks me, is that the wee cow that hit you, mumbling and scared I reply yes dad that's her, that's the girl. My father then tells me to fuck off and get out of his sight as he shouts my sister into the living room.

My father tells her, you better go outside and beat up that little bitch, and if you don't do it, I am going to give you a beating, for not defending that little sissy of a brother.

My father gets such a kick out of watching us fighting, and he encourages it at every opportunity.

My sister has no choice but to go out and fight with Karen; the only other option is to get a beating from my father.

Forced to go outside and fight, I watch from my bedroom window, and I can see my sister approach her.

My sister tells Karen; this is for hitting my little brother, and grabs her long-pleated hair, she swings Karen around with such force that Karen's feet come entirely off the ground. She then lets Karen's hair go mid-swing, and Karen flies through the air, landing on the concrete pavement. As Karen hit the pavement, she rolled along the ground, scraping her arms and legs, she then leaps up crying and runs off toward her house.

A few minutes pass and Glenda arrives at our front door, she is livid and starts to shout at my father, look at my Karen, it's disgusting what your daughter has done. You should be ashamed of her, can't you see all the marks on my Karen's knees and arms, as she points out the grazes. My father just stands in the doorway, staring right through her as she shouts at him, he patiently waits until she finally finishes. My father then sniggers and says, are you finished, I'm glad you've managed to get all that off your hairy chest, now why don't you fuck off away from my door, then he slams the door on her face.

A few days later, my mother bumps into Glenda at the school, and they begin chatting about the whole situation. My mother is a peacekeeper, and the conversation goes on for ages, by the end of them talking, my mother and Glenda have resolved the situation, and have become friends. My mother's conversation with Glenda gives me time to chat with Karen, and this is the start of mine and Karen's friendship.

During the summer, our friendship grows, I am up early and out playing with Karen all through the summer holidays. Karen is a very spoiled child; she has every toy you can imagine and always a full drawer of sweets in her bedroom. Glenda makes sure to keep Karen's sweet drawer full, preventing any behaviours. If Karen's treat drawer is not topped up, she becomes a problem child, and no one wants to deal with that.

This summer is one of the best summers ever, Karen and I get up early every day, and we are out playing by seven o'clock. We go around in the morning with an old guy called Jack; he collects all the rubbish in the local area. Jack is an excellent old guy, with grey hair and a little Jack-Russel that always follows him around everywhere. Jack is so kind to Karen and me, he tells us all sorts of adventure stories, and on our route, he gets us a chocolate bar from the shop. He is like a sweet old grandpa to us, and we thoroughly enjoy our time with old Jack.

We go out in the morning with Jack, and then in the afternoon, we play in the maze or go up to the river. Karen always runs off as soon as the streetlights come on; that is her alarm call to go home for her shower.

I don't have a set time to be home at night, and always wait out late with the older kids, I learn a lot from them, as they tend to get up to stuff. They have sex in the bushes, or under the bridge, they get drunk all the time and take drugs, it is all done in front of me. I never want to go home; I know my father is going to be there, and there is always some fight going on with my parents.

The holidays are soon ending, and everyone on the street is talking about going abroad on holiday, and all of the new toys they have got. I secretly wish I am one of them, with their beautiful homes and holidays, all I have is Karen, Jack and the river where we play.

I'm glad I have Karen and Jack there for me, and not just the older kids, as I could undoubtedly go down the wrong path in life very quickly.

Before the holiday's end and the school returns, myself Karen and my sister are collecting Acorns, Chestnuts and Pinecones from the trees at the river. Out of nowhere with no warning, Karen swings the bag of nuts and smacks my sister full pelt right across her face, then runs off. I have no idea why she hits my sister; it is just random.

When we return home, my father can see the red mark across my sister's face. He asks, what happened to your face? After telling him, he is furious with Karen and tells us that after his shower, he is going to that old cow Glenda's door.

As my father steps out of a shower, he looks out the window and catches a glimpse of Glenda walking past. He starts to shout obscenities from the second-story window; he is calling Glenda for everything. Then Glenda looked up and replied, you know Ronald, you might scare your wife and kids but not me.

Glenda's actions set my father off like a firework, and he goes into a rage. Picking up the large, heavy vase that is sitting on the centre of the living room table, he launches it full force right through the window at Glenda. The glass goes everywhere, and Glenda just calmly looks up at my father, shakes her head and laughed at him. My father is infuriated by her, and he goes completely crazy, he starts shouting abuse through the smashed window and saying to her, I will get you, your nothing but a nosey old fucking witch, you think you are so fucking smug. He is screaming so loud at her, and then he stomps off to his room and starts looking out his clothes to get dressed and go after her.

Within minutes a police van pulled up outside the house, and two rather large officers come to the front door. The police ask him if they can enter the house; he is still going crazy; however, he allows the officers to enter. My father is shouting and says to the officers; I take it that nosy old bastard called you to me. The officers speak to my father very calmly and say Mr Proctor; we are only here to keep the peace, and to make sure that the children in the house are ok. My father realised the situation he has caused, and he calms down. The police then say to my father, Mr Proctor; we can see the children are safe and you appear to be calm now, I take it we will not need to visit again after we leave. My father reassures the officers there will not be any more trouble, and he shall clean up all the glass; however, he makes it clear to them, that he is the innocent party. He says it's all that Glenda's fault, she knows just how to get under my skin, she just wants to get a reaction out of me, and I have given it to her.

The police then leave the house, sitting outside in their van for a good while, before they eventually leave the street.

My mother and Glenda don't talk for a long time after the police have visited our house. I can't say the same for myself and Karen; It only took a few days before we are back out playing together. I asked Karen, why she smacked my sister with the bag, she just said I have no idea Callum, I just had this urge and could not hold back, something inside me told me, I just had to do it.

The summer holidays are now over, and I'm back at school and devastated as there is no escape from my father. I am back to sitting at that table in the kitchen with my homework, no more hiding from him. My father firsts name is Ronald, and the older kids in the street have realised my father is quick to wind up, so they start walking by our windows and sing songs. I've just come down from the Isle of Skye, I'm not very big, and I'm awful shy, oh Ronald, where's your trousers. They sing it over and over. The singing of the song winds my father up terribly and makes it a difficult time for our family to be around him. My mother is struggling already, and now my father turns his frustration to her because of their stupid song. Every day he is in such a mood shouting and screaming at us because of their singing.

I'm now eight years old and starting back to school, and I'm in primary five. I have a new teacher, Miss Frazer, and she is lovely and very kind and gentle with all the kids, she likes to give us reading homework, she says it stimulates the brain.

Every day I sit up the river on my own and practice my reading, I read it over and over until I have memorised it. I have to learn my reading word for word before I return home, as my father has rules for our homework. If I make too many errors during my homework, I get punished.

Rule 1. On arrival, homework placed onto the kitchen table.

Rule 2. Do not move from the kitchen table until all homework is complete.

Rule 3. Read the book from beginning to the end, not just the allocated pages from the teacher.

Rule 4. If you make a mistake, start the book from beginning again.

As I sit on the stool next to my father, he tells me to start reading the book from the beginning, and I am so nervous with him sitting there right next to me.

On this specific day, the book I am reading has the word new year in it. I'm doing well with my reading, and I'm already halfway through the book when my father slams his hand down on to the table; and shouts no, now start from the beginning.

I start over, and each time I get to the word new year, my father slams his hand on the table and makes me start over. I am unsure where I am going wrong, and I make sure to read every word very carefully. Several more attempts fail, and once again, I get to the part that said new year, and my father punches me full force off of the stool.

I don't know where I'm going wrong and start to cry, and my father tells me, if you don't stop that crying, I will give you something to cry for, do you want the belt? Now sit down and start from the beginning.

I am so confused, and I think I'm reading it correctly, I reach the words new year again, and my father grabs me by the throat. He picks me up off the stool and is choking me in mid-air, I'm panicking, and I can't scream or breathe. Then he throws me across the kitchen and starts shouting at me, are you doing it deliberately? Do you think I am stupid? Are you trying to take the piss out of me? As I cry, I stutter at him; dad please, I don't know what I'm doing wrong, I am reading all the words correct, please I don't know what I'm doing wrong. My father lunges across the kitchen and grabs me by the scruff, he lifts me off the floor again, and pulls me right up into his face, he starts shouting its new year, not fucking new yea. It is then I realised; I have been saying the word wrong, I am saying new yea, instead of a new year. I have not pronounced the r on to the end of the new year. He says, now once again start from the beginning, and if you mess it up this time, it will be the belt you get; now read it.

I started over, and as I get to the new year, I have this slight pause in my voice. I'm shaking with fear, and I can hardly see the writing as my eyes fill with tears, I am trying to hold my tears back. I know my father will beat me if I cry, luckily, I get it right, I am so relieved when I finish my reading and get myself out of that kitchen.

I remember one time during reading homework; he hit my sister on the back of her head with an ashtray for getting it wrong. Homework time is so scary, and I hate having to do it, I'm not sure why my father is so strict about it, perhaps he just enjoys the power and control.

My father is always shouting at me, and it's not only at homework time, but it is every day. He says things to me like; you are as thick as shite, you will never amount to anything, you are so stupid, just look at you your no use to anyone. Nothing I ever do is good enough for him, and every day I get this bombardment of insults.

I find myself becoming jealous of the other kids in the street, as their parents are taking them swimming and going to football matches, even going on holiday. The other kid's parents did simple things, like take their kids to the park or giving them a couple of quid for the ice cream van. It would be a rare occasion if my father did anything nice for me. If he did do something kind, it would be in front of official people, like teachers or social workers and that's all just pretentious to make him look good, and not because he cared.

My father decided he is going to take me on a day trip to a Castle. I am so excited about going on a day trip with my father; he never went anywhere with me, and he knows I have a fascination with castles and forts.

My father makes sandwiches, a flask of tea and some biscuits, and off we go.

As we walk around the castle, I'm having such a fantastic day with my dad, looking at the old armoury, the walls, and the castle dungeons. When we reached the very top, my father gives me some lunch, then asks me, to come over to where he is standing and look at something, he tells me that I will like what I see. He is standing over in the corner at the very top of the castle, and not thinking, I just run over and look down, it is the cliff edge and a sheer drop to the rocks and sea at the bottom. It is a terrifying drop, and as I am looking over the edge, my father walks over and asks did you see that unusual thing right at the bottom. As I take a second look-over, my father clutches the back of my coat and pushes me. I am hanging over the cliff edge, and my father's grip on my jacket is the only thing preventing me from falling. I try to pull myself back in; however, he is too strong and holding me out over the cliff edge. He starts to laugh at me because I'm panicking and begging him to pull me back in. He keeps laughing at me and says, just think Callum I could kill you right here, and people will believe it is an accident, I can tell them you climbed up and fell over, who will know the difference. I am so terrified I think he is going to drop me over the edge, so I start screaming as loud as I can, so he then pulls me back in. Then he says, I took you here to show you just how easy it is to get rid of you, and I don't want you ever to forget this day.

When my father finished hanging me over the cliff edge, he takes me straight home. He never spoke to me all the way home, and I am confused as to why he did this to me, was it just to scare me or did I do something wrong, I don't understand.

The castle and the cliffs

Other than loving castles and forts, I have a fascination with outer space. I have all those little toy stars and stuff that glow in the dark, and I have stuck them all around my bedroom. I also loved sitting outside on the pavement for hours and hours just looking up at the night sky; I would sit there wishing a spaceship would fly past and take me away.

It is my birthday, and my Grandmother has purchased me a cracking big white telescope, and gave me a space book, telling me where things can get located and where to look in the night sky. I am so happy with my present, and I spend hours looking through it at the moon and space; I just love it.

I've now had my telescope for a few months, and I'm in my bedroom looking through it when I hear my father loss on his computer game, he is shouting at the computer. Our living room is directly below my bedroom, and I listen to him throw something across the room. It hits off the wall and sounds like it has broken, then I heard him get up, he starts to stomp toward the living room door, then he thumps up the stairs toward my bedroom. As my father gets closer to my room, he begins to shout, getting louder and louder; I am terrified, I have nowhere to run, and I know he is coming for me. He just keeps screaming; You think you are smarter than me, and you think you can put me off my game, well I'll teach you to be so fucking smart.

Trapped in my room, with nowhere to run, I just freeze like a statue, standing there staring at the bedroom door, and waiting for him. As my father enters, he batters the bedroom door open with such force the handle gets stuck in the wall, he lunged across the room, trying to grab me. I am so scared, I just dropped to the floor and curl up into a little ball, I am screaming, don't hit me, please dad, I'm sorry please don't hit me. He punches me several times, then he grabs me by the front of my pyjamas, lifts me off the ground, and screams into my face. It's a strange noise; like he is imitating a baby crying, he is mocking me. My father then shakes me back and forth up in the air and throws me onto the floor; I am screaming in fear, pleading with him and begging him not to hit me.

He stops, turns to walk out the room; I am lying on the floor, relieved and thinking it's all over. When my father notices the handle of the door got stuck in the wall, he clenches his fists and puts them on to his head, letting out this mighty roar. He starts shouting again and saying, look what you've made me do, as he turns toward me, he picks up my telescope and raises it into the air. I begin screaming again; please, dad, don't hit me, I'm sorry, I will be quiet. He does not care and smacks me with the telescope; he keeps beating me with it over and over. I try to protect myself by curling into a little ball, and I just keep pleading for him to stop; finally, he stops when the telescope brakes into bits. He then yells at me, that will fucking teach you to be so fucking noisy, you're not so fucking smart now, now clean up this fucking mess and keep the noise down.

When he leaves my room, I'm as quiet as a mouse and try to fix my telescope. I can't do it, as he has damaged it beyond repair, so I quickly tidy my room then go outside, and I stay out of the house for the remainder of the day.

My father is cunning; he makes people think he is a nice and decent man. He always acts differently when in people's company and is sure to present himself well. He gets smartly dressed and polishes his shoes, just like a military man, and appears to be this caring father and husband. When indeed he is only fixated on how others see him, and he gets so angry with us if we do anything that might embarrass him.

On this occasion, I have received an invite to a friend Claire's birthday party. Claire stays on the same row of houses, four doors down. It is exciting for me, and I am looking forward to the party. I have never been to a proper birthday party before; I had my little parties in the house with family, but nothing outside of the home. My father makes sure I ware my best clothes; I have my new shoes, little grey trousers and a white shirt and tie. I am clean and tidy, and my mother has gelled and styled my hair, I feel so proud in my new outfit and my hairstyle, I am very hyper, and I am so looking forward to the party. My father is very strict about our behaviour when we are in the company of any adults. He pretends our family do better than we are; he never wants anyone to know that we are struggling through life, and we have no money.

Just before I'm ready to leave for the party, my father tells me you need to know the rules before you go.

Rule one no making a pig out of yourself, I do not, want people thinking we don't feed you.

Rule two do not touch anything that does not belong to you.

Rule three if you make a show of yourself, it reflects poorly on me, so behave and do nothing to make an idiot of yourself.

My father then asks, do you understand me? I am dismissive of his question and quickly reply yes yes, I know, I need to behave and not make a pig of myself. I am so excited to get out of the house and go to the party, and I don't realise what I'm saying.

Then my father tells me, Callum, you have the choice; you can wait in and not go to the party, or you can take the punishment before you go, so I know you won't forget my rules. I am unsure what he is saying to me, and have gotten myself so hyper and excited about going, I just answer without thinking. I choose to go to the party, please, please I want to go, can I go?

My father looks at me with a shocked look; he said ok go into my bedroom and get me the black belt from the dresser.

As I walk into his bedroom and pick up the black belt, I suddenly realise what my father is saying to me. I feel complete dread as I pick up his belt, and as I go back into the living room and hand it to him, I say I've changed my mind. My father looks at me and says; it is too late, you've made your choice, now drop your trousers and your underwear. He gripped the shoulder of my shirt, then positioned me in front of him, took his belt and whipped me three times across my bottom. I started to yelp, and my backside is red raw and stinging; it is so painful.

My father tells me to fix myself and says take that as a warning, and if you do anything to embarrass me at this party, you will receive another three when you get home.

When I arrive at the party, my bottom is still on fire. However, I quickly forget about the pain, as I glance around the room, I am mesmerised; there are balloons and banners everywhere, and lots of presents on the table. Over in the other corner is a massive table against the wall with a mountain of sandwiches, sweets, juice and cakes. Claire's mother approaches me, and she tells me to help myself as she pointed to the table on the far wall. I instantly think about what my father has told me and chose not to touch any of the food and treats. I pick out a single chair in the far corner of the room, and I sit on the same chair for the entire party. I don't move an inch and never get involved in any of the games, and I don't eat any food or talk to anyone. I am too afraid I will make a mistake, and if my father finds out, he will give me the belt when I get home. As the party is coming to an end, my father appears at the door to collect me, I'm terrified, and listened to every word as Claire's mother talks to him. She says Callum has been as quiet as a wee mouse, and he never ate a thing, I do hope he is not coming down with something. Then she says, I hope you don't mind I made this little goody bag with some treats, and a slice of birthday cake, it's for Callum to take home, he has been great, and I don't want him to miss out.

As I arrive home, my father is ok with me, he tells me, don't eat all of that shite Claire's mother gave you in one, or it will make you sick, and don't even think about eating it before your dinner. I am so happy that I don't get the belt when I return home.

I get invited to go to more childhood parties, and they were all the same; I would go and sit quietly and not move from my seat. I never get involved in any games or eat any food for fear of getting the belt from my father, and I dread receiving invites to parties and hate going to them.

On this morning, I have awoken to my first wet bed, and I am so scared, I do not want to tell anyone. I know my father will be angry, as I have soaked the sheet and the mattress, so I try to hide it. I take off my wet pyjamas and placed them flat under the duvet cover; I then make my bed back up as if nothing has happened. I wait until my father has gone out, then I talk to my mother, I start to cry and say I'm sorry mum, please don't be angry, I have wet my bed, and please don't tell dad; he will get mad at me. My mother is understanding, and she says, you don't need to worry, I'm not angry with you, these things happen, it's just a little accident. We both strip and wash my bedding, aired the mattress, and after a while, remade my bed. My mother looks over to me and says, the problem is now solved, see there is nothing to worry about, no more wet bed, lots of children have little accidents, and it's ok. I feel such relief.

When my father returns home, I can hear my mother telling him what has happened; she said Callum wet his bed last night and did not want to say anything, he is scared of you and was trying to hide it. My father replied, it's just laziness, he needs to learn to go to the toilet. I am shocked; I expected my father to be angry and shout at me; it is like he did not care, I felt ashamed of myself, and at the same time, I felt relief my father has not got mad at me.

My bedwetting continued; it is not every day; however, every so often, I would have a little accident and wet my bed.

In the beginning, my father accepts my bedwetting, and he is civil to me; however, as time progresses, he decides it is time for me to stop. His first approach to preventing me wetting my bed is to shame me. He tells me that if I wet the bed again, I will have to wear a nappy, I assumed I would be wearing the nappy to bed.

The next morning, I have wet my bed, my father walks into my bedroom, he throws a nappy at me, and tells me to put it on. My father makes me wear the nappy throughout the day, at first wearing the nappy never bothered me. It's not until My father tells me I must go outside wearing it. He wanted the other kids in the street to see the nappy and tease me, encouraging me to stop wetting my bed. It is so embarrassing and soul-destroying getting forced to go out in front of the other kids in the street. By chance, my mother's sister, Auntie Gillian, is passing and sees me, she approaches me and asks, are you ok. I get embarrassed and tell her about my father making me wear the nappy, and how it is upsetting me having to wear it in front of my friends. My Aunt asks, where is your father? I say I think he is in the house playing on his computer.

She is furious with him and marches right in the front door; she has a right go at my father, I can hear her from outside shouting, although can't make out what she is saying to him. I expect my father to shout me into the house and give me into trouble when Aunt Gillian left; he never, and he never forced me to wear that nappy again.

My father never mentioned what my Aunt said; however, it is evident my Aunt Gillian has made him angry at me. She may have stopped my father, forcing me to wear that nappy. She only made matters worse, and my father starts to force me into a cold bath every time I have a wet bed. He tells me it will teach me to keep my mouth shut in future. He is not content with just cold baths and says to me if you can sleep in that bed soaked in your pissy sheets, you won't mind wearing wet clothes. He then forces me to wear wet clothes straight from the washing machine. The wet trousers and jeans make me break out with a rash on my thighs and inner legs, stinging severely in the cold weather, the pain is so distressing for me.

My sister is only a few years older than me, she is very strong-willed, she never shows any fear towards my father, and regularly stood up to him. On several occasions, my sister tells my father he needs to stop making me wear wet clothes; she tells him it's wrong and cruel. My father appears to listen to her, and after a while stops forcing me to wear wet clothes; however, he continued with the cold baths.

My father became determined that he will stop me wetting the bed, telling me that the next time he will take my piss-stained sheets and hang them out of the bedroom window for the whole world to see.

The next time I wet my bed is on a school morning, my father being true to his word, at the interval with everyone in the school playground, takes my sheets and hangs them from my bedroom window. It is upsetting for me, and he has humiliated me in front of the entire school. My bedroom looked on to the school playground and the football field; it is not long before all the kids realised what my father has hanging from my window and start pointing and laughing. For the remainder of the interval, I hide in the school cloakroom and cry. When the school bell rang, I returned to my classroom, and the kids in class start to tease me. My father never hung my sheets out the window after that day; however, it is too late; his actions have caused me to get bullied in school.

I come up with a solution to my bedwetting problem; I will not sleep. If I don't sleep, then I can't wet my bed, I start to stay awake as much as possible, splashing cold water on my face every hour. If I need to urinate, I'm awake, so there is no chance of going in my bed. On the weekends, I try to catch up with as much sleep as possible, my plan works, and my bedwetting is limited to weekends. I start feeling exhausted during the week and falling asleep in class, and I nod off for short periods at my desk. The teacher is continually coming and banging her hand down on my desk and asking, Callum, are you still with us. As I am forcing myself to stay awake, I become so tired and can't focus or concentrate on anything, and I just want to sleep all the time; I am exhausted.

Once a year, the school send out report cards, and When my report card gets delivered, it stated. Callum does not pay attention in class, he is easily distracted, and he is a daydreamer.

My teacher requests a meeting with my parents, she informs them, due to the reasons given on Callum's report card his schoolwork has suffered. She then recommends extra homework, to assist me with getting up to speed with the rest of the class.

My father never once thinks my lack of concentration is because of him; he decides to give me the belt and tells me it will teach me to pay attention in class. Thanks to the teacher insisting that I get more homework. I am now even more stressed than ever, forced to sit at that kitchen table and do homework, and knowing I am going to get smacked if I get it wrong. There is no escape for me; it is like a vicious circle.

CHAPTER FOUR

Age 9 to 10

_____

THE TRIP WITH
A *WET BED*

My mother is struggling to cope, and everything is getting too much for her. Bringing up three kids, and one with a disability, the new house, my abusive father, and her father, who is an alcoholic, it is all taking a toll on her.

A good friend of the family has come to visit my mother. As they chat, she suggested that my mother seek help, explaining there is a charity run organisation that can help, and it's entirely free. The charity is there to help families that are going through hard times. At first, my mother is apprehensive, afraid the social work department might deem her unfit, and try to take her kids away.

After talking some more with her friend, my mother agrees to get the help, so her friend helps to contact the charity, by making all the necessary calls and arrangements. Once everything got completed, it's just waiting to hear back from them.

After about a month my mother received a letter, it is from the organisation, they have two places left on the bus. They ask my mother to complete the documentation enclosed and return it to them. My mother's friend comes to the house and helps with the paperwork, and now it is just waiting for my sister and me to go away on holiday.

Our holiday is fantastic news, my sister and I will get away from the house for a week, and my mother will now have the time to look after my baby brother Steve. Steve needed so much after-care due to his operations, and he is visiting the hospital regularly. With my sister and I on holiday for a week, my mother will get a well-deserved break, two mouths less to feed and run after.

The day has arrived, the charity does a local pick up from all the kid's houses, so my sister and I get our little cases ready and go outside and wait at our gate. While waiting on the minibus, I begin to feel nervous, this is my first time away from home, so my sister reassures me everything is alright.

As the bus approaches, I can see it is full, and we are the last kids to get picked up. Luckily, I have a seat with my sister, and I can chat with her until we reach our destination.

The charity group has taken us to an outdoor centre for kids, and the centre is in the middle of nowhere, nothing but water, hills and trees for miles. As it is the first time my sister and I have ever been on holiday, it feels strange being away from home, however, when we arrive the guy in charge, Phil, makes us feel welcome. Phil is excellent and gives us a tour through the building, there are lots of fun activities, and the place looks fantastic. Just as I start to feel comfortable in my surroundings, Phil walks us into a dorm and shouts, right girls you are all in this dorm, pick your bunks and get unpacked.

I suddenly have this feeling of dread fall over me and realise I will not be sharing with my sister. I am going to be sleeping in an unusual place and surrounded by strangers who I do not know. I had forgotten entirely about my bedwetting problem until now.

It was rare if I wet my bed, but it still happened on occasions, and I'm so nervous having to share a dorm with all the other boys, and not my sister.

On the first night of the holiday, I try so hard to stay awake; I think, if I stayed awake, as I had done at home, I would not wet my bed. However, with all the excitement and travelling, I am exhausted and fall asleep. As soon as I wake, the first thing I do is examine my bed and pyjamas; it is all dry, I feel such relief waking up to a dry bed, it gives me such confidence. The place is now like a breath of fresh air; knowing that my father is not about, makes me feel safe, and having a dry bed is a bonus.

On the first morning, we have toast and beans for breakfast; it is strange being around so many other kids, and knowing my father is at home, I could relax and not be scared.

After breakfast, Phil takes a group of us down to the river; he asks everyone to line up on the river's edge. Phil then shouts, right kids listen up, as your great ancestors did before you, this is where we shall wash today.

The water is ice cold, myself and all the kids start to get washed, everyone is screaming it's too cold and splashing each other. The cold water doesn't bother me; I'm used to from the cold baths my father puts me in.

After everyone gets washed and dried at the river, Phil shouts, I hope everyone had fun washing in the river. I can't wait to see the fun you will have climbing that hill, as he points toward a massive hill on the opposite side of the river.

Phil then splits us into two groups and challenges us; we must build a stone bridge across the river, then climb the hill and return the flag from the top of the peak to camp. The day is fantastic, and everyone works together as a team.

A few days into the holiday, and I am having the time of my life; the place is excellent; I am thoroughly enjoying all the outdoor activities. Then the worst thing happens, I wake to find I have wet my bed, I panic and start to think my dad will find out, and he is going to kill me. I began to think about Phil and all the other kids sleeping around me, I know I'm going to get punished for this, and the other kids will all laugh at me as they did in school. I just lay there waiting for everyone else to leave.

About fifteen minutes pass and most of the others have got up and left the dorm, then Phil comes in and looks around the dorm, he said in a joking manner, ok guys last chance to get up or no breakfast. Some more guys get up and leave the dorm; this left another two boys and me. I am feeling embarrassed and just wish they would get up and go.

Then the strangest thing happens, Phil walks back into the dorm and closes the door, he says, its ok boys the coast is clear, you can all get up now, but no one moves we all just lay there looking at one another.

Phil then tells us a heartfelt story about his childhood and how he wet the bed in his youth, he says it is common among kids, and that we should never be ashamed of who we are. The penny suddenly drops, I'm not the only one who has wet my bed. I realise the other two boys have also wet the bed, and one of them is much older than me, so I suddenly feel like I am not alone.

All three of us get out of bed and go into the shower room, we all strip down then get washed, everything is so silent and not one of us utters a word.

After the shower, we all go back to the dorm to get dressed, still not a word is spoken; we just give each other a glance, nod and smile. We respected each other's privacy, and we never spoke of it again. Wetting my bed that day, I am very embarrassed; luckily, it never happened again for the remainder of the trip.

The place has a huge outdoor play area for kids; it is incredible, so my sister and I go outside to play on all the equipment.

I have a higher-pitched voice than most kids my age, but I never give it much thought. However, one of the boys in the camp approaches my sister and me; he is much older and bigger than me. He says to me, why do you talk like a wee girl? I answer, what do you mean? He replies, what do you think I mean? Are you a little poof or fag or something? My sister instantly pushed between myself and the boy and asks, what's your problem? Then she tells him to go away and leave us alone. Without hesitation, he punches my sister square on the nose; it is awful, she is screaming, and her nose is burst wide, there is blood everywhere.

I get scared, and run as fast as I can, telling the guide what has happened. Once my sister gets cleaned up, the boy responsible receives a speaking too; however, he is allowed to stay at the camp and mix with everyone.

My sister and I don't enjoy the last few days of our trip, that boy had ruined it by punching her in the face and bulling me. I am however glad we went on the trip; it makes me realise, I am not the only person to have a bedwetting problem, and that it is ok to have an accident now and then.

Returning home from the trip, my father heard about the incident with the boy punching my sister in the face. He gives me such a hard time for not sticking up for myself and my sister; he never beat me on this occasion; however, I think that would have felt better. He ridicules me for several days, calling me a wee sissy, he said I am a coward for leaving my sister, and I should be ashamed of myself.

As I am passing my father in the hall, he pretends he is going to punch me, I flinch, and jump to one side, he laughs at me and mocks me, telling me, I'm nothing but a wee sissy. He keeps the insults coming, saying, I can't hit back, I make him sick, I need a girl to fight my battles, and no wonder people think I am a wee poofter. His insults are consistent, and every day he belittles me.

Summer has now passed, and winter is fast approaching, at Christmas time I don't receive big expensive presents, always the small things. My mother tries her best; however, money is short, so I make do with what I get, and I appreciate it. What I did not know is this Christmas will be the best Christmas of my childhood. My mother always takes all the presents out the night before Christmas and places them under the tree, then my sister and I feel all the gifts, and we try to guess what they are. Then my mother permits us to open one present on Christmas Eve night, the rest we unwrap on the morning of Christmas Day.

Christmas morning, and I'm up and out of bed like a shot. I race downstairs and look through all the presents; I separate the ones with my name tags attached, noticing my pile is substantially smaller.

I begin to open all my gifts, and it's all the usual stuff, Socks from my Grandmother, an apple, an orange, a curly wurly and fifty pence from Nana Rose; A He-Man figure filled with bubble bath from Papa Mack, and some selection boxes from my other Aunts.

I am so happy, and I have opened all my presents, now I sit watching my sister open hers; I am thinking about how my sister's pile is massive compared to mine. My mother asks Callum, is that all you got? I just smiled at her and said its ok mum. My sister then looked over at me, smiled and said, mum, we can share mine; I have lots. My mother then leans over to me and hugs me, telling my sister no Beth, you don't need to do that, Callum has his own. She says the thing is Callum your other present never fitted under the tree; my face lights up with a huge smile, my mother shouts to my father, you can bring it through.

My father pushes the door open, slides this huge box over to me, I spring to my feet and start ripping off all the paper. It's the BMX bike I have always wanted; I'm over the moon; it's even in red, my favourite colour.

After everyone has finished with the presents and cleared the mess, my father takes me outside and helps me to ride the bike. Having my father teach me to ride my bike, makes me feel proud, for the first time, I am that kid, I am out in the street with my father by my side. I want the world to see my father helping me; it is a unique moment, and I feel just like one of them now.

As I learn to ride my bike, in the beginning, I need to use stabilisers. However, I am a pro in no time, then my father takes the stabilisers off, having the bike gives me a bit more freedom, and I cycle everywhere. Every day I am out on my bike, going adventures and exploring new places, and I go that little bit further each day.

Not long after Christmas, and like usual, I want to go out and play on my bike, I run to the window checking the weather, the sky is bright blue, and the ground looks crisp with frost.

As I open the front door it is freezing, I can see my breath in the air, I see the icicles hanging from the roofs, and the ground sparkled with frost, it looks beautiful.

I get on my bike and start peddling like crazy, I'm darting up, and down the road, which is next to the river, and in the winter the river became a deadly force.

I am not paying any attention, and up and down the hill I go, trying to go faster each time. As I go down the road, out of nowhere, an ambulance appears, it comes speeding around the corner toward me, and I'm cycling like crazy going as fast as possible.

As the ambulance approaches me, I veer off to the left side, trying to avoid it. Then as I pull my breaks, the ice causes my bike to keep going, I lost control and the bike skids into the kerb, causing the bike to flip with me still on it. I start to tumble down the embankment and land face-first in the rapidly moving water, my bike lands right on top of me. I'm panicking face down in the water and can't breathe, the bike is pinning me down, I have no way to get out, and I'm gasping for air. Struggling, I manage to get one hand onto the riverbank, grabbing around trying to get a hold on something, but there is nothing but loose mud. I keep slipping back under the water, I'm so tired and frantically grabbing at everything and anything.

My neighbour, Mr Parker, grabs hold of my arm, and yanks me right out of the water, he seen everything from the opposite side of the river, and he climbed down to help. I'm so scared I thought I was going to die, my clothes are soaking, I'm freezing, and covered in mud. Mr Parker looks me over and asks, are you ok? Gasping, I reply yes, I'm ok, thank you for saving me, he then smiles at me and says, you are one lucky boy.

Mr Parker then helps me to the top of the riverbank and takes me home, explaining to my mother what has happened. My mother says to me, your fortunate that Mr Parker was there to save you, then asks me to thank him. She then tells me; I could have easily drowned and that I should go upstairs and get out of my wet clothes.

On returning to school after Christmas, I don't have many friends, and it's a hard time for me, things have got worse, and the bullying continues. This one particular boy, he won't stop picking on me, and the other kids decide to join in with making fun of me. I'm sure it's because of my father hanging my bedsheets out the window and making me wear that nappy, he might as well put a big target on my back that said, bully me.

Although I don't have many friends in primary school, Karen has always been a true friend; she is continuously there for me.

I am standing in the playground, and this girl Lizanne decides to have a go at me, she walks toward me and insults me. I'm confused as I have not done anything to make her nasty to me; I hardly even speak to her. Lizanne starts to sing a song at me, something about me peeing the bed and smelly wellies, so I argue back with her. She has this little potbelly, so I tell her she needs to look in the mirror and go on a diet. Lizanne doesn't take kindly to my comments, and in a rage, marches right up to me, and smacks me full pelt across the face with a yellow piece of washing line; she was using as a skipping rope. It is painful and stings like crazy, my face has this instant raised loop on it, the mark is on my cheek for about two days, and I have to hide it from my father.

After telling Karen what Lizanne has done, she becomes furious and tells me she will get Lizanne back for hitting me. I ask Karen not to do anything, as I am scared, it will make things worse. Lizanne has an older brother, and I don't want him coming after me.

The next day, I see Lizanne, she has scratches and a bite mark on her face, I try not to stare at her, but it is apparent she has got attacked. When I meet Karen later, I ask, do you know what happened to Lizanne's face? Karen says, let's just say, I've made sure she will not be hitting you again.

A few days pass, and everyone at school is talking about what Karen has done to Lizanne. There is a rumour going around that Lizanne's friends, the twins are going to retaliate against Karen. The twins are feared and always fought as a team; they are tough girls and also very close to Lizanne.

During the interval, I could hear much noise coming from the school shelter, and I knew it is going to be Karen. Someone shouted over to me; it's the twins, they are going after your friend Karen for hitting Lizanne. I am concerned for Karen, and I felt guilty; this is all because I insulted Lizanne, Karen is going to get beat up and hurt, and it's all for defending me.

As I arrive at the school shelter, there are so many people gathered around the girls. I can't see what is happening, and everyone is shouting and encouraging them to fight. As I push my way through the crowd, I hear Karen screeching like a wild animal, and I can also hear the twins, they are both screaming at Karen.

When I eventually get through the crowd it is too late, the fight is over, the twins had cornered Karen in the shelter, and there was no way out for her. As they started to attack her, they quickly realised it was the biggest mistake they made, Karen lost all control and beat both of them. She had them both pinned on the ground by their hair; she just kept kicking in at them. One of the twin's hair got pulled so hard, Karen had ripped it out, and the clump was laying on the ground next to them. When Lizanne new the twins had no chance against Karen, she had run off and told the teachers. All the teachers came running out, and it took three of them to stop Karen, once the fight got broken up, the twins walked past me with the teachers. I can see both of their faces are in a terrible state. I never had any problems from the twins or Lizanne after that day, not one of the girls in school ever said anything to me after Karen took care of the twins.

The boys are a different case, they all have decent clothes, most of their parent's work and they have things in common with each other. I have nothing in common with them, I have a high-pitched voice, my family has no money, and I am terrible at football. I lack confidence in sports, and because of my father, everyone knows I wet the bed, so no one wants to be my friend.

It seems every day a new person has something to say to me, Pissy pants, mink, poof and the list goes on, it is constant.

One day I go into school, and a boy walks up and punches me in the face, for no reason, his friends find it funny, and they all laugh at me. It becomes a regular occurrence to be insulted and bullied, one time, I even have drawing pins put on my chair, and gum stuck in my hair. It is too much, and I am too scared to tell my parents about what is happening at school, I fear my father will ridicule me, or worse beat me for not defending myself.

When I am alone at night in my room, I lay in my bed crying and asking myself, why are all these horrible things happening to me.

On this day, I'm sitting alone in the playground, and I can see all the boys standing in a group, they are pointing and sniggering over in my direction. I'm not sure what they are looking at, to begin with, I thought they were pointing at the girls. Then one shouts over, alright Michael Jackson, are you going to do the moonwalk today, I suddenly realise, it's not the girls, it's my socks. I have no clean black socks in my house, so my father told me to put white socks on, it looks terrible, my black trousers were too short, and with black shoes, my white socks stood out like a beacon.

I want to get out of there, and if I can get around to the other side of the building, I can hide in the cloakroom. No one ever goes into the cloakroom, so I know I will be safe hiding in there, but the only way is to walk through the boys.

As I start to walk through the group of boys, one of them tries to trip me, and he failed, then one of the boys pinged a sweet at my face. My adrenaline is pumping, and I'm angry, but at the same time to scared do anything. I feel this thump on the back of my head, and it dazed me for a second, I suddenly realise one of them has just punched me, and they are all laughing at me.

I'm not sure what snaps inside me at that moment; however, I just see red, I turn to the boy, I scream at him, do it again, go I dare you, hit me, go, go. I then punched myself in the face and yelled at him, do it, hit me, do you think I care anymore. I think I startled him for a second; then he looked at me like I am stupid; then started to laugh at me, all his friends followed suit. I am so furious, I grab him by his tie, and I punch him as hard as I can, I smacked him right on his cheekbone, and he fell to the ground, and everyone stopped laughing.

I walk away and hide in the cloakroom for the duration of play-time, as I sit in there crying my adrenaline is pumping. I'm nervous, shaking, and proud, all at once, I have finally stood up for myself.

The day after I punched the boy, he came into school with his parents, he has a huge black eye, and I feel fantastic, I have finally stood up to them.

The boy's parents complain, and I get into trouble from my teachers. However, my parents don't give me into trouble; my father just tells me it's about time I started to hit back, and stop being such a little sissy.

Things change in school after that day, and I am glad I stood up to that boy, as bullying has reduced substantially, sometimes it still happens but not like before and not physical; I think seeing me lose my cool makes them think twice about picking on me. Karen and I are very close in school, and she is the perfect Ally, I think most kids in school are afraid of her, including the boys.

My first ever experience with a girl is with Karen, we are in her bedroom, and both playing picnic with a tartan blanket and a plastic tea set. It's fun as we have all of the sweets and cans of juice from Karen's treat drawer. Then we change the game to doctors and nurses, and we are both pretending to bandage each other. Then we ask each other questions about our private parts, which leads to showing each other. We touched each other a couple of times and explained the sensations; it is nothing sinister, just two kids being curious.

Karen's mother keeps passing the room door every five minutes to put washing away, and It is making me nervous. We both know we should not be doing it, and I tell Karen I think we should stop, and just play until I go home. We don't speak to each other about what happened in the room after that day; however, I do think it gives us a closer friendship bond.

Things at home are starting to look up, my parents do not seem to be arguing as often, and school is getting better, things seem to be on the right track. My father starts working for my Uncle josh again, doing a night watchman job, and my mother gets some peace with him out of the house, and now we have some extra money coming in. I think having the extra cash puts my father in a good mood, as he has not hit me in a good while. He is even being kind to me and asks if I'd like to do a night watchman shift with him, I jump at the chance, this can be my time to make my father proud, and I can get to explore a building site.

It is an eventful evening, as soon as I arrive on the site, I go off on my adventures. I am having so much fun; however, it is freezing, so after a time, I go back and sit in the work van. We have a flask of coffee, egg sandwiches, and some biscuits, I fall asleep pretty fast after my coffee. During the night I get awoken by an older man banging on the van window, I'm startled and look around for my father, but he is gone. The old guy is drunk, and I can't understand him; he is trying to tell me something. He just keeps banging on the van window and telling me to open the door; I am shouting at him, go away, leave me alone, I don't know you. I have no idea who he is or what he wants, so I begin to panic, and I think my father has left me. At that moment, my father appears at the side of the building; he is doing his rounds checking the site. My father shines his torch on the old guy's face, then shouts over to him, Algy what are you up to mate. My father knows him; they spoke for a bit, and then Algy staggers away. It turns out old Algy works on the site, and he was trying to give me a set of keys, that he had taken home by accident, and after a night at the pub, he decided to return them.

Later that night, my stomach starts to feel slightly uncomfortable, and I think It is possibly the coffee or the egg sandwiches from earlier. As I go back to sleep, my stomach starts to grumble and ache, so I tell my father, and he says it's probably just trapped wind, don't worry about it, once you pass it, you will feel better. I quickly realise it's not only wind, I accidentally have a loose bowel movement, and the diarrhoea gets everywhere. Everything just comes away from me, it's all over the seats of the van, and my dad is livid, he is shouting at me, and telling me to hold it in. The work van is stinking, and my father is cursing me, telling me I am disgusting, he drives me straight home telling my mother to make sure I scrub myself. It is such a cold night, and even with the windows down, all I can smell is my diarrhoea. As I leave him in the van to finish his work, it had such an unbearable stench; I'm sure my father must have hated the rest of his shift.

CHAPTER FIVE
Age 10 to 12

WHEN MOTHERS OUT

One night my father comes home, he has been out drinking all day and most of the night. Both my parents get into an argument; it goes on into the early hours and is pointless. They just kept going over the same things again and again, money, debt, not having any shopping, and drinking. Then came all the personal attacks on each other sides of the family. The only thing stopping my father from being physical that night is the fact he is just too drunk to get up. Eventually, my mother went to her bed, and my father passed out on the sofa with half a bottle of Bacardi by his side.

The next morning my mother is up early, and she leaves the house with my sister and baby brother, I am unsure where she has gone, or when she will be back. Having my mother out of the house feels like an eternity. The whole house is a mess and smelled like a brewery, and I am stuck in that mess with my father.

My bedroom is located on the top floor, next door to the bathroom. I am sitting in my room, playing with my toys, I can hear my father, he has finally woken up and is coming up the stairs, not giving it much thought I just continued playing. First, he went into the bathroom and used the toilet; then, he started to run his bath. I can hear him pottering around, he keeps coming in and out of the bathroom, hovering around at my bedroom door and heavy breathing. Something is not right, he is behaving strangely, and it makes me feel very uneasy.

Then my father asks that I go into the bathroom; I have this terrible feeling of dread, and I don't want to go in there. I pretend I can't hear him, so he shouts again, you get your ass in here. I'm coming I answer, as I walk into the bathroom, my father closes the door behind me. The bathroom is long and narrow, and he is standing behind me; he ushered me past the sink towards the toilet and away from the door. I know something terrible is about to happen, so I start to cry. My father asks, why are you crying, I have not even done anything yet, as he bends down toward me, smiles at me and pressed his face against mine kissing me. First, he kisses me on the cheek then turns my face to kiss me on my mouth. It is disgusting, I can feel his breath on me, he stinks of the stale alcohol, and I can feel his stubble and moustache on my face, I feel sick and scared, and I just keep crying. He wipes the tears from my face, and says, now that wasn't so bad. I don't speak, and I just looked down at the floor.

My father then stands up, putting his finger under my chin, and lifting my head to look up at him. This time the smile fell from his face, he opened his bathrobe and said in a stern voice, now suck it. I start sobbing, and pleading with him, please I will behave, I am sorry, please don't make me. My cries make no difference, and he just pushes my head towards his privates and said now suck it, put it in your mouth and suck it. I am frightened, and I have no choice, so I do what he asks. As he becomes more aroused, he turns me around and starts to rub himself against my bottom. He is touching my privates, and at the same time began to push hard against my anus with his privates. It is excruciatingly painful, and I start screaming at him and begging him to stop. My father then stops trying to force himself into my anus and keeps me facing away from him. He continued to fondle me and masturbated himself until he ejaculated onto my bottom. My father then tells me to go to my room and wait for him.

When I get out of the bathroom, I consider running away; however, I have nowhere to turn. I am already in what is supposed to be the safest place with my parent and have no idea where my mother is, or if she is even coming back.

I am terrified of my father, and there is nothing I can do, I am only ten years old and have no chance against a fully grown man.

After my father has his bath, he came into my bedroom; I have not moved from the same spot the whole time, crouched down in the far corner of my room with my head tucked between my knees crying. He calmly walked up to me and said, do you remember that time at we visited the Castle, the time you almost fell over the cliff. Well if you tell that's what will happen to you, and if you say anything to your mother, it will be the last thing you ever say. He then says to me, look at me when I'm talking to you and asks do you understand me? I lift my head, and nodded slightly then tucked my head back between my knees. My father then walks out of my room and acts normal, and I'm sitting there in my room all alone and a total nervous wreck, now I'm even more terrified of him than I have ever been.

I don't leave my mother's side after that day; I stick with her like glue, where my mother went, I would follow. If I know she is going out somewhere, that I can't go, I make sure I am out of the house before she leaves. I will sit in the park or hide up the river, and I will wait out all day into the evening, that way I know she will be home before I returned. If my mother is in the house, I can feel safe, and after what my father has just done to me, I must make sure I will never be left alone with him again.

About six months have passed, and nothing has happened. I have become an expert at ducking and diving from him, I have managed to avoid him for all this time.

Then one day my father says you can wait in with me today; your mother has got too much on, she has got to get the shopping, then she is going to see your Nana Rose. I immediately want to get out of the house. I fling on my shoes and head for the front door; my father shouts where do you think you are going. I say I'm just going out to play, he looks at me and says not in that whether you are not, today you can wait in with me. I become hysterical, and I get overcome with panic and fear, I know he is going to do it again. I beg my mother; please take me with you, don't leave me, please don't go, I don't want you to go, and I'm grabbing on to her. My mother says to me, stop this carry-on, I'm only going for some shopping, then on to visit your nan, I will not take long. When I realised, I can't go with my mother, or go outside; I hide under the washing basket-like it is going to protect me.

As soon as my mother is out the door and he is sure she is gone, he locks the doors and goes upstairs to run a bath. I'm still hiding under that washing basket, I'm so quiet, and I listen to every movement in the house. My father then shouts for me, and my heart sinks. I don't speak a word, and I just keep quiet, I'm as still as a statue hiding under that washing basket. He yells again, except this time he makes a whipping noise from his belt, and shouts get up these stairs. I don't want to go up, but I have no choice, I'm only ten years what chance do I have against him, and he has locked all the doors. I have nowhere to go, and I can't get out, so I slowly start walking the stairs toward the bathroom. It feels like an eternity, and I know what's going to happen, I can feel my whole body shaking with fear. When I reach the bathroom door, I just breakdown crying and begging my father not to do it.

My father prompts me to enter the bathroom, and then he closes the bathroom door as soon as I'm in there. He tells me to move up next to the bath, I'm sobbing and begging him, no please, please dad, I don't want to, please don't do this to me again. My father ignores my cries, and he does not care as he forces me to strip naked, pulling my pyjamas off and putting his privates into my mouth. I am so scared, and I'm crying, begging him to stop. He says to me, just do as I tell you, now be quiet and just suck it, he then tells me what he wants me to do with my mouth and tongue. My father gets angry with me, and he starts to shout at me, you need to stop your crying, you are not doing it right, so stop your fucking whining, you need to suck it. I just can't stop sobbing, and as my father is not getting what he wants from me, he tells me to stop. He then makes me put my privates into his mouth, and he sucked and fondled me, as he masturbates himself. I'm crying the whole time and asking him to stop, but he does not care. He just continues to masturbate himself until he ejaculates, then like before, he tells me to go and wait in my bedroom.

I can't stop crying; I just walk from the bathroom to my bedroom. I go to the far side of the room and curl up on the floor, I am laying there for ages sobbing; and eventually, I fall asleep.

My father later comes into the room and wakes me; I am still laying on the floor; he sits down next to me on the bed and starts to cry. My father tells me, he is sorry for doing what he has done to me, it will never happen again, and he did not mean to hurt me.

My father then asks me to sit next to him on the bed. I am so scared and do what he asked, then he reaches for me and hugs me. Callum son, he says, you can't say anything to anyone about this. The social workers will come and take you away from your mother, and you will never see your mother or sister again. Your mother will be so angry with you for breaking up our family, and he makes it clear I can't ever tell anyone. I feel so frightened, and I am apprehensive about trusting him, I believed he meant what he said, as I have never seen him cry, I am convinced, he is telling me the truth. I did not want to lose my mother and sister, so I keep quiet, I just hoped he is telling me the truth and stops, and it is over now.

It seems my father is true to his word; months pass, and he has not sexually abused me. However, I am always on edge, knowing it can happen again at any time. What never stops is his physical and mental abuse, and one of his favourite things is making my sister, and I fight.

On this day, he makes us push the sofas to the edge of the living room and move any other furniture out of the way. He then placed some items in a pile on the middle of the floor, a hairbrush, a belt, a plastic spoon and a shoe. He then tells my sister and me to select one of the items; we both grab for the biggest hardest thing, I got the large serving spoon, and my sister got the hairbrush. Once we have our weapons, he tells us to sit back to back in the middle of the room; my father sat on his chair, his chair is in the far corner of the room, his game is that we fight each other.

However, the fight has rules.

The game rules.

Rule one, we can't stop fighting until my father tells us to stop, rule two, No biting and rule three, No hitting on the face.

Once sitting back to back on the floor, he shouts fight. We both stand up, turn to face each other, and start fighting, kicking and punching at each other, pulling hair and choking each other, and thumping each other with our weapons. My father just sits back on his chair, and he is shouting at us, kick him in the nuts, punch her in the guts, go on smack her, use your weapon. My sister and I knock lumps out of each other, it goes on for a long time, or until one of us gets hurt, we are not allowed to give in, we must fight until he said stop. My father tells us that by making us fight, it teaches us to stand up for ourselves, but I think he just likes watching us hurt each other.

I am always too scared to tell anyone about him making us fight, or the abuse and sexual abuse. My father makes it clear I can't ever say, and if I did, there would be consequences.

On this day, my father enters my room, he wakes me for school and is quick to notice I have a wet bed. My father grabbed my hair and pulled me from the bed; he strips the bedding then tells me, to get myself downstairs and put my pissy sheets into the washer. My father is still shouting as I walk down the stairs, I don't want that piss stinking out this house.

When I return upstairs, he is running a cold bath for me. He shouts me into the bathroom and tells me to get in and scrub myself. He goes into my bedroom, banging around, and slamming my drawers while getting my clothes ready for school, he is in such a rage. I then hear him stomp passed the bathroom and go downstairs.

No more than a minute could have passed, when he starts shouting from downstairs, move it pissy; you are going to be late. I quickly come out of the bath, and I'm shivering and begin to dry myself when he shouts again, am I talking to myself; move your fucking ass. I don't finish drying off, just quickly start to get dressed and walk into the hall toward the stairs. He shouts again to hurry up, and I'm still fastening my clothes as I begin to run down the stair. I'm so nervous as I reach the bottom of the stairs; he is standing waiting for me. As I go to pass him, he slaps my face, then he smacks me hard across the back of my head, knocking me to the ground. He is still shouting at me, saying when I fucking tell you to move, you move, don't dilly dally, he throws the front door open and shouts, now get to fuck, move it, get yourself to school.

I am so upset; I can't stop crying as I walk to school, and I can't take it anymore. My class has already gone in when I arrive, I walk in, and my teacher looks over at me, she can tell by my face something is wrong, and asks me, are you ok? I started wailing uncontrollably, so she takes me outside the classroom. I tell her everything, and I'm going at 100 miles per hour, blurting it all out, stuttering and sobbing. He hits me, cold baths, beating mum, touching me, nappies. My teacher crouches down to me and says, Callum, please calm down, and will you please come with me. She escorts me down to Miss Mcclusky's office; the headteacher; she asks me to sit outside and wait, while she talks with Miss Mcclusky in her office.

While I am sitting outside, Miss Mcclusky decided to phone my father, she tells him, you have to come into school, your son is in a terrible state, and we need to talk to you.

Our house is only yards from the school; my father is there so fast; both teachers are still in the office discussing everything when my father arrives. My father sat down beside me outside the office, and it is only myself and him. My father looks at me; he had this look of rage on his face, he asks, what have you said to them? I told my teacher you hit me.

Sitting there with my father, I am terrified; he takes a grip of my hand; he holds it so tight and started to squeeze it. He then said this is what you are going to say, you have made this whole thing up, it's because your brother is in the hospital, and you feel left out, do you understand me? I replied with a nod. My father then said, god help you when you get home, for opening your big mouth, it's going to be the belt, do you hear me? Then we just sit in silence.

Miss Fraser came out of the office, and she looks surprised to see my father there so soon, and she invites both of us into the office. My father sits there, right by my side, and says he is so sorry about this whole mess, and that he knows what is going on with me. My father looks directly to Miss McCluskey and tells her; it is all our fault as parents, we are spending far too much time with Callum's little brother Steve. We have been going back and forth to the hospital, it has been non-stop with Steve, and it has not been easy on the family. Due to the circumstances, we have not given Callum any attention since his brother went into the hospital.

I get forced to sit there with my father by my side and say, it is all my fault, I just feel so left out, and that's why I made up this whole story, I did it for attention. My father then tells me to apologise to the teachers for wasting their time and then intentionally said to me in front of them. I have not to beat myself up about it, and he will be giving me a bit more attention now. The Head Teacher then gives me a telling off she went on to say, I should understand my brother is sick, and I should be helping my parents, not causing them more grief, by making up stories. She then says I have wasted schools time and drones on about the importance of education.

The entire experience is awful, and I have nowhere to turn, and I feel trapped and alone. I wish I maintained my story for the teachers and told the truth about what he is doing to me. It was just too intimidating with him sitting on the chair right next to me. There is no way I would talk out against my father, not with him sat right there. My father must have gone over what he would say, should I ever talk out, he was so prepared and direct with his answers. He precisely knew what to say and made it easy for the teachers to believe him.

As I arrived home from school, my father is waiting in the kitchen, and he tells me to go straight to my room and says he will be up when he finishes his cup of tea. I go straight to my room. I sit there on my bed; only a few moments pass; however, it feels like an eternity.

I am sitting in my room nervously waiting on him, and I start to daydream out of my window, I'm running through things in mind trying to come up with something, so he would not beat me. He batters my door open, entering my room with a belt in hand, I instantly snap back to reality.

I start to cry, please don't hit me, I did not mean to tell, I won't do it again, I promise, I've learnt my lesson.

He raised his voice and said, I think it's a little too late for that, don't you, you have already opened your big fucking mouth, I warned you this would happen, now I will teach you to keep it shut. He grabbed me by the scruff, yanked my school trousers down, and leathered my bare bottom with the belt. He lashes me about eight times in quick succession; it is so painful. My father shouts as he leaves my room, you won't be going out today, get your pyjamas on and bring any homework to the kitchen table.

As I get changed into my pyjamas, I look at my bottom in the mirror; it is stinging like crazy, and scarlet red, I could see the raised red whip marks on my legs. He has hit me to low down and missed my bottom; I thought the pain would never leave me; it lasted for such a long time.

I took forever to put on my pyjamas; I don't want to go downstairs as my bottom is still very sore. I am afraid I will get punished again if I mess up on my homework.

As I enter the kitchen, my father is already sitting at the table with a cup of tea. I slowly walk toward the wooden stool; my bottom still hurts, and I find it challenging to sit. I started to read and make a few small errors; however, my father is lenient with me. I think my father could see my pain and discomfort sitting on my stool. When I completed my homework, he said, have you learnt your lesson about opening that big gob of yours, I looked at him and replied, yes and nodded. I think my father is feeling guilty for lashing me with his belt when he knew I told the truth, as he then says, I believe you have learnt your lesson, after your dinner, you can go out and play. I go straight to my room after my homework and never came out until the next day, I am in far too much pain.

My father played things very smartly that day with the teachers and made them feel sorry for him. The way my father responded is perfect; no one suspected him as a beast for a minute. While he walks away unscathed, I have received a lecture, lost any credibility I have with them and also received a lashing from my father.

Six months have roughly passed from the incident with the school. Although my father is still physically abusive to me, I have not been sexually abused by him for some time. I believe I had deterred him when I spoke out to the school. I don't care that I have lost my credibility and got a whipping from him; it is all worthwhile if it makes the sexual abuse stop.

It is not long before I discovered the real reason why my father has stopped with the sexual abuse; It is nothing to do with my speaking out.

He has received a letter with a court date; it is for Peg Legs trial.

My father knows I will have to talk to court officials; I will be going over my initial statement regarding Peg Leg.

The court case is making my father very nervous, and If I spoke out this time, my father would not find it so easy to wriggle his way out. This time, it is law enforcement officers I will be talking with, not a primary school teacher. As time grows closer to the court date, the more helpful and caring my father becomes. He acts like a different person to me, buying me little treats and giving me money for the ice cream van. He talked to me and treated me like a proper person, the way a parent should treat their child.

Time passed fast, and there is a tension in the air, I have my eleventh birthday, but with a court case looming over everyone, no one is in the mood for celebrating. My father is extra nice to me, with the police and social workers coming and going from the house for Peg Legs trial.

My father has nothing to be worried about, I already got let down by my school, and my father has bullied me physically and mentally into silence. I am too scared, and I am never going to speak out; he has shut me up.

A year has gone passed, and Peg Legs court date has come, everyone in the house is running around like crazy. My father is on his phone, trying to arrange transport to court. Both my sister and I are making sure we look presentable, and my mother is tending to my brother, who won't stop crying.

My father purchased new clothes for my sister and me; he wanted us to look our best for court and his family, he makes it clear we had better not give him a showing up. With all his family being there, he wanted to be sure we have our fake smiles and pretending to be the perfect family in front of everyone.

When we arrive at the court, I could feel the tension; everyone is acting strangely, groups have formed, and everyone is whispering to each other.

Suddenly there is silence in the room, as everyone looks toward the door; as Peg legs family just walked into the same waiting room. Everyone is outraged; there is confusion why they are in the same area. Peg Legs family appeared to be embarrassed; I don't think they had expected to be in the same room; the families never approached each other. A member of our family asks the court officials, why they were there, it turned out they have made a case against Peg Leg and also wanted him prosecuted. Our family knew now that Peg Leg has sexually abused his own family; there was mutual respect toward each other. It appeared things stacked against him, and he will be going to jail for a long time.

All of a sudden, there is commotion and noise, word quickly passes around the room, Peg Leg has turned up to court with my Grandmother at his side.

My Grandmother must have decided she will stand by him, and it is devastating for the family. The family had hoped my Grandmother would change her mind and support her grandchildren. However, by walking in with him, she has made it clear, she has chosen him over her own family.

During the commotion with Peg Leg entering the building, a lawyer approached my father with a folder, with our statements in it. He wanted us to read over them one last time before entering the court. However, the lawyer has given my father the wrong folder, and it has everyone's statements in it, and not just ours. My father sees everything; all of the charges brought against Peg Leg, there are more charges against him than we first expected. It is due to this mix-up that I know Peg Leg has raped my cousin in the bathroom that day we all played hide and seek.

The court case doesn't take long as Peg Leg pleads guilty to twelve accounts of sexual abuse on children, and several other charges.

As he pleads guilty, we were all spared having to go into the courtroom and give our statements. Peg Leg received two years of good behaviour, ordered to visit a psychiatrist, and placed on the sex offenders register. The justice system had failed us, and Peg Leg won't spend a single day in jail for his monstrous crimes. He is a free man and making it worse, my Grandmother stands by him through it all, so the family disowned her. We all live in the same community and see Peg Leg and my Grandmother regularly in the streets, and at the shops.

Things never took long before Peg Leg is back at his old tricks, family friends spotted him on my Grandmother's mobility scooter. He is hanging around the primary school at finishing times and watching the children as he waits at the school gate. Peg Leg would entice the children to go for a ride on the scooter; he deliberately keeps sweeties in the front; he used the sweets to encourage the kids to sit on his knee. As the kids sit on his knee, he prompts them to ask their parents to go a drive around the school grounds, he then drives them around the school, and once out of sight from the parents fondles himself with the kids still in the scooter.

When my family discovered he has been giving kids rides at the school, we knew something sinister must be going on; Peg Leg has done the same to children in the past. My sister is infuriated and decides to go to school at finishing time; she approached him; she lost her cool and started to shout at him. One of the mothers at the school approached and said to her, stop yelling at that poor man, he is disabled, he is here waiting on someone, he is harmless. The parents were none the wiser; all they could see is a vulnerable man with a scooter and presumed he is waiting on his grandchild. My sister explained to the mothers; he is a registered sex offender; what he is doing is trying to groom your children.

The mothers reported him to the police, and he received a warning to stay away, Once again escaping a jail sentence. After that day, Peg Leg never returned to that school; however, there is just no way of knowing if he went to another school.

Peg Leg and my Grandmother's house became the target of abuse from the local community. The word is out that Peg Leg is a registered child predator, and the local community are outraged. All the windows in their house regularly get smashed, and the front of the house got painted, with the words, A PAEDOPHILE LIVES HERE; it is bright red and in capitals. The garden got vandalised, and the mobility scooter stolen and dumped into the river.

I feel pity for my Grandmother, and I don't understand why she chose to stand by him over her grandkids, even after knowing the atrocities he had committed.

Some time passes, and my family find out Peg Leg has taken a seizure; the seizure is so severe it has killed him. My Grandmother continues to live in the same house after him passing; we still never spoke to her; she lived a long lonely life. When the community discovered Peg Leg has died, they have no reason to bother my Grandmother, and they left her in peace.

I am now twelve years old, and I have started to get confused about my sexuality. As I am growing up, I get teased a lot about the way I speak; I have a high-pitched voice, and the other kids in school say I am gay because of it. My father is always calling me a wee sissy. With everyone always telling me I'm a poof, I'm a gay boy, and a little sissy, I started to think that perhaps I am.

I begin to look at boys differently, and most of my friends are girls, the boys don't want to hang with me, because they are scared, I will make them look gay. Throughout the summer, I start to feel more and more attracted to boys; It makes me feel sick inside; I don't want to think or feel this way. I begin to blame my father for making me feel gay, and I keep telling myself it's just a phase, I think there is something wrong with me, and I resented myself for feeling this way.

There is a boy in my class at school; his name is Ian. Ian lives just a short walk from Karen and me, and he is one of those kids that will hang with you if there is no one else, and if the boys appeared, he would be off like a shot to play football. Despite him running off when something better came along, he is always very kind and friendly to me, and he never made fun of my voice. Sometimes if it started to rain, Ian would invite me to his house to play with his games. I enjoyed being in his company, and he is a nice guy.

We have just finished primary seven together and will be going into high school after the holidays.

On this day it is raining, so Ian invited me into his home. He wanted me to play with his wrestling figures; we were having fun and started to practice real wrestling moves on each other. Ian accidentally touched my manhood and apologised; he then did it a second time. As we continued to wrestle, we got very close and then started to kiss. At which point, Ian's mother shouts for us to wash our hands as she has made us some lunch; we just looked at each other and started to laugh.

Ian then said, well, are you coming down as he ran off downstairs to the bathroom, and I followed. As we are both washing our hands, Ian smirks at me. Then he splashes some water onto my face, I laugh and splash him back, we then leaned towards each other and kissed again, this time not just a small kiss, but a proper long kiss. It is strange and slightly uncomfortable; we stopped when his mother shouted, letting us know our sandwiches were ready. I'm not sure why Ian kissed me, and after eating lunch, we watched some tv, and then I went home. I felt confused and excited about what has happened and nervous about seeing Ian again.

The next time I see Ian, I say hello with a big smile; However, he completely ignores me. I feel embarrassed about the whole thing, and I get red-faced every time I see him, even when I see him alone, he ignores me. Ian never spoke to me again, and I hate myself for what has happened, and I rebel against my feelings of being gay.

CHAPTER SIX
Age 12 to 14

THE BREAKUP THEN
The Break Down

Over the past year, things have gone from bad to worse. My mother is barely coping with three children and struggling badly with the abuse from my father, and now she finds out she is expecting a fourth child. I think she worries about her pregnancy as my father had beaten her during her the pregnancy, and nothing is stopping him doing it again.

I believe the beating's my mother received from my father when she was pregnant last time, is the cause for my brother's disabilities, but I can't prove it.

My mother makes the only decision she feels she can; she chooses to walk out on him. She decides to move in with my Nana Rose and live in her small one-bedroom cottage, meaning no room for my sister and me. She can only take my baby brother; However, my mother promises me that when she is re-housed, I can go and live with her.

The house feels so empty without my mother, living there with only my father is difficult, especially at Christmas time, it's just horrible.

My father has no clue what he is doing, and we still have no money and no food. Without my mother running hand and foot after my father, it is starting to take its toll, and he can't cope with all the cooking, cleaning, washings and getting us up for school. He knows he will lose a good thing if he lost my mother.

Christmas day and my father gives this big speech to my sister and me. He says, Christmas is not about presents and riches, it is more about our family being together. Still, your mother has chosen to take your brother and leave us, so this is not me doing this to our family, it is your mother. She is the one breaking this family up; she has caused this mess, and you can both tell her that when you see her.

The house feels so empty without my mother, living there with only my father is difficult, especially at Christmas time, it's just horrible.

My father has no clue what he is doing, and we still have no money and no food. Without my mother running hand and foot after my father, it is starting to take its toll, and he can't cope with all the cooking, cleaning, washings and getting us up for school. He knows he will lose a good thing if he lost my mother.

Christmas day and my father gives this big speech to my sister and me. He says, Christmas is not about presents and riches, it is more about our family being together. Still, your mother has chosen to take your brother and leave us, so this is not me doing this to our family, it is your mother. She is the one breaking this family up; she has caused this mess, and you can both tell her that when you see her.

Christmas dinner that night is very different, my father has decided we will eat dinner in the living room. He said the tv is good, and there are lots of Christmas movies showing, and he wants us to watch them and eat together as a family.

I am sitting there on the sofa, watching tv and patiently waiting on my Christmas dinner. When my father enters the living room and hands me my dinner plate; my jaw drops, the contents of the plate are two king ribs, and that is it. They are way overcooked, and there is no veg, two king ribs and a cup of tea that is my Christmas dinner. When My father saw my face drop, he reminded me to be grateful as there are people out there starving, who have nothing.

After dinner, my father said it's all your mother's fault anyway, if she hadn't left you, you would have had a decent dinner, and things would be different, I am doing my best.

Many months have passed before my mother finally gets her own house. Her new home is a three-bedroom house in a respectable area, with a seven-year waiting time for council houses, it's the desired area to be, with a good community and all good neighbours. My mother got housed there so quickly because she is now a single parent, and my brother has disabilities.

I am happy for my mother, she has stood up to my father and now managed to get a new home of her own, I too can now get away from him.

My father is very manipulative, he knows just how to play my mother, and she is vulnerable being pregnant with a fourth child on the way. Things are tough for her, being alone and trying to bring up three kids, one with a disability, and trying to refurnish and decorate a house.

My father worked on my mother every day, begging and pleading with her to get back together, he continuously bombards her with phone calls. He swears to her he will never hit her again; he will change and make things right this time.

My father starts back working for my uncle Josh, it is on the side, and he is still claiming from the government. He begins to splash the cash in front of my mother, buying things, and offering to help my mother with bills. Then he passes his driving test, convincing her a car will make life easier for them. He tells her things can get better, and all she must do is take him back.

One day he turns up at my mother's door, said he had been offered a swap out of the big house to a small flat, the woman is willing to pay him five thousand pounds if he swaps with her. My father used this to his advantage; my mother never had much in her new house, the bare minimum, and some rooms have no carpets or furniture. My father promises her the world; he said he would use the money to help fix up her new house; all she had to do was take him back and let him move in.

Baby number four is born, it is another boy, and my mother is exhausted.

My father has pushed and pushed her until my mother broke, she has given in to him; however, she did make terms for them getting back together.

1. My mother keeps her house; it also stays in her name.

2. My father completes the swap then gives up his own home and moves into my mothers.

3. My father helps out with the house and pays his way as he promised.

4. If my father lifts his hands, he is out for good.

My father accepted the terms laid out by my mother, and they get back together. He wastes no time moving in, and I'm devastated, my life is better without him.

I am now twelve years old, living in a new area with zero friends, I'm about to start high school, and my father moved back to live with us. After kissing Ian, I'm confused about my sexuality, and my mother just had a fourth baby. Now the doctors have diagnosed my Nana Rose with terminal cancer.

My father has become a loving husband and is buying my mother new carpets and new furniture for her house. My parents even receive some good news, my brother will receive the highest rate of disability money, and all the payments will get backdated.

We now appear to be rolling in the cash, with my father getting a wage from Uncle Josh, and claiming his benefits money, and the five thousand from the house swap, along with the backdated disability money. Everything appears to be less stressful; my parents even seem to be getting on, and the food cupboards are always full. My father decided to get a new family car threw the disability, and my parents even start having nights out together. With this new steady cash flow, everything is going so well, and It is not long before baby number five is on the way. It looked like my father's fake charms worked, he is back, and he is here to stay.

As time passes the five grand and all the backdated disability money starts to dwindle. In the short time my parents have cash, they grew customary to it. The cupboards being full, going for drives, smoking forty cigarettes per day, and the money quickly disappeared. My parents start to go back to all the debt collectors, borrowing money to keep up with the new lifestyle. After a few months pass, now they have to start paying all the money back.

My parents managed as my father still had a job with Uncle Josh. However, soon that ended, and now my parents could not afford to pay all the debts they had run-up, bringing much-unwanted stress back into our home.

My father appears to try his best, but with the added stress of no money, his attitude starts to change, and he slowly turns back to who he was. He begins grinding my mother down again, its small things at first, with passing comments, he would say something like; are you going to eat "another" slice of that cake? I think that outfit makes you look fat, don't you? I see you got your haircut; don't you think it looked better the other way, and maybe you should put a little bit more perfume on tonight.

My father is always saying things to make my mother feel low, over time, his continual subtle insults work. My mother has become very low, looking after five kids. Then she gets diagnosed with postnatal depression for a second time, it's just too much for her.

When my mother thinks things can't get any worse, she received the terrible news, my papa Mack, also has terminal cancer. Now both my mother's parents have the disease, and there is nothing the doctors can do.

The whole experience is heart-breaking and pushes my mother to her limits. After a long fight, my Nana Rose dies first, a short time after Papa Mack followed, it is devastating for my mother.

During my mother's time of mourning, my father continued to make her feel bad; making out the situation our family is in was all her fault.

My father started to say regularly; everything was ok when I lived on my own; you have wasted all our money decorating this shitty place. My father is relentless with his cruel comments, and he starts to pass remarks to suggest she is a bad mother. Saying things like, did you let the kids go out looking like that? What kind of mother does that? You look terrible, how are you supposed to take care of your kids if you can't even look after yourself? He just keeps going, never letting up on her.

My mother has a mental breakdown with both her parents passing, and my father continually grinding her down. She could no longer cope and got admitted to a psychiatric hospital.

Things get hard with mum in the hospital, and with me being the new kid on the street, the other kids start bullying me right away.

The street split into two groups; one group is all the rough kids; they are into everything, including drugs and drink. The second group are not as mischievous, all their parents have good jobs, and they are proper posh kids.

My first encounter is with a couple of the kids from the rough group. They have this ringleader named Rab, Rab is a few years older than all the other kids, he is a proper bully, and all the posh kids knew to stay well clear of him. Rab has a sidekick named Daz, and the two are inseparable.

One evening, as I am coming home from the shop, I have to pass through the alleyway to get back. I can see Rab and Daz are both standing in the alley, and it is evident by their behaviour; they are both intoxicated or on drugs.

As I approached them, I try to walk around them, and nervously, I look at them and say hi, Rab stands right in front of me on the pavement, blocking me from passing, then he says, what have you got in that bag mate? I say stuttering, eh, it's just my dad's stuff; it's just some shopping. Daz then snatches the bag from me, as Rab pushes me away, stopping me from grabbing the bag back. Daz starts to rummage through the bag and takes out a carton of milk, then says, can I have this mate? I answer, come on guys it's my dad's stuff, please I don't want any trouble, Daz then opens the milk and pours it out all over the pavement. Daz then reaches into the bag again, this time he pulls out the jar of sauce; and says, I guess I can't have this either and he smashes it onto the side of the road, both just started laughing at me and walk away.

I have to tell my father something; there is no way I can tell my father the truth. Telling him will just make him mad, and he will force me to go out and fight with them, or he will beat me then argue with their parents, either way, it will make things worse. I decided to make up a story, and tell him there is a gap in the kerb at the alley; I say I fell in the hole and twisted my ankle, and the sauce and milk smashed as I fell. My father believes my story, then gives me more money to go to the shop, telling me to be more careful. As I walk to the shop, I am vigilant and listen out for them, luckily Daz and Rab have disappeared, and I manage to get the shopping home safe.

The other group, the posh kids of the street, in the beginning, they never said anything to me; they just kept their distance. The posh group can tell our family hasn't much money; I don't have the designer clothes as they do, I guess 'that's why they don't want to be my friend. The posh kids have a ringleader; his name is Jake, and he is so horrible to me. Jake is a big boy, and I don't want to cross him, he always passes comments whenever I walk past their group, and all his friends laugh. The bullying escalates from our street, then to school and on the school bus.

When on the bus, they would flick stuff at me and say stupid things deliberately loud enough so I can overhear them. Something like, do you think Callum is a gay boy, I think he has a boyfriend, and he's a stool pusher, can't you guys smell the shite,

I got told his mother's a looney, I hear she's in the nuthouse. It becomes constant, so I decided to start walking back and forth to school.

With my mother in the hospital, things are not getting any better at home. My father is in the living room playing on his computer; I can hear him cursing and shouting and throwing things around; it's because he is losing. I am lying in my room, I have been here all day, and I'm so hungry. Still, I dare not get up for something to eat, I know if he sees me, he will blame me for losing at his game, so I just lay there and eventually fall asleep.

Suddenly I am awoken with this massive pain in my stomach, I can't breathe, and I'm gasping for air, my father is shouting something in my face. He has lost on his game and got angry, came into my bedroom and punched me full force in my stomach; he has caught me off guard and knocked the wind out of me as I slept. He then grabs me around my throat and starts to strangle me, and I can't breathe. With his hands still around my throat, he pulls me from my bed shouting at me, you're a wee fucking bastard, 'you're a wee fucking jinx, I hate you, it's all your fault, then he lets my throat go as he throws me back down on to my bed. My father then storms out of my room and bangs the door behind him, shouting you're grounded. I just lay there in shock and crying; I'm trying to figure out what just happened. I don't sleep for the rest of the night, and with the slightest noise, I perk up and become alert, terrified he will lose again and burst back into my room.

The next morning, my father is in a terrible mood; he has been up all night on his computer and stuck at the same level. I can hear him from the bedroom; he is banging about and slamming doors and drawers in the kitchen. The house is tense, and my baby brother is continually crying in the living room. I hear my father stomp from the kitchen into the living room, he slams the door with such a bang, and in a rage starts to shout at my baby brother. Shut the fuck up, will you just shut the fuck up, and give me a fucking rest. My baby brother stops crying briefly;

then, he starts to cry again.

My father then shouts for me to come through to the living room, he is attempting to change my brother's nappy, and he tells me to go to the bedroom and get some cream. With my mother in the hospital, my father is struggling big time. My baby brother keeps crying and will not stop, so my father loses it and goes into a complete rage, picking up my baby brother and shaking him back and forth. My father is screaming into my brother's face, telling him to shut up; he then throws my brother across the room onto the sofa, then he picks him up and with force starts to slap him. He whacks him full force, repeatedly across his bare bottom and legs, and shouting over and over, shut up, shut up, just fucking shut up. My father has struck my brother so hard you can see the red handprints across his bottom and back.

My father then shouted at my sister, you better get your arse in here and shut that fucking thing up, and while you are shutting it up, you can change it. Then he went back to playing his computer game. My sister becomes the mother figure after that day, she does everything, while my mother is in hospital, the cooking, the cleaning and looking after my three brothers and me.

A few months pass and things have not gotten any better, and my father decides to let us visit my mother in the hospital. I'm missing her terribly, and so excited about going to see her.

It is a long drive to the psychiatric hospital, all the way there I sit in the car thinking about everything that's been happening at home, and how much I miss my mum. I envision that my mother will be waiting for us, and I will run up and give her the biggest cuddle.

When we arrive, things are not what I expect, as soon as we enter, there is a waiting area at the front door, and a large desk with several nurses sitting around it. There is also a long corridor with rooms on either side, and my mother is nowhere in sight. My father leaves us in the waiting area and tells us to watch the tv while he talks with the nurses.

My sister and I are waiting, and my father with a nurse walks along the corridor into a room. While my father is in the bedroom a man comes running past, we can see him through the window. He is looking at the ceiling and shrieking, no words just shrieking, over and over until two nurses at the desk take him away, and escorted him along the corridor into a room. A second man with bandages on his wrists walks into the waiting room and sits down next to me. He starts uncontrollably crying and saying, I tried to kill myself, but they stopped me. Next time they won't be able to stop me then he sits there just giggling to himself, and telling my sister he is pregnant. He is an enormous guy like a giant; I don't utter a word, just sit still and stare at him. Two nurses quickly entered the waiting room, prompting the big guy out the door, and down the corridor and into a bedroom.

After a few more minutes passed, my mother walks out of a room with my father; she comes into the waiting room and looks exhausted. I give her a massive cuddle, and I keep staring at her; she looks completely different. She says I've missed all of you, how are you all getting on. I look at her and ask, why was that man shrieking, and the other guy crying? She sits down on the chair next to me and says, well like mother, they are not well, and just like me, they are in here because they need a rest. That big guy, the one that was crying, he used to be a professional wrestler and is just very down now. The other guy, he is an artist and just needs some sleep, and then he will feel better.

Anyway, enough about them, I want to hear from you, how is everything at home? My sister comes right out and tells my mother the truth; things are not good, my father hit our baby brother, he flung him across the room and slapped him. My mother just gives my father a look of disgust, then turns to us and says, I know things are not great with me in here, but I will be home soon. I promise everything will be ok, and I just need you all to be capable until I'm home. We chat for a short time, then we all hug my mother before my father walks her back to the room, where my parents have a private chat before we leave.

During my mother's time in the hospital, the doctors have given her a vast support network. My mother talked with the doctors and explained the situation at home, telling them my father is struggling to cope and that he needs some support. My mother is reluctant to say too much, just enough to get my father some help.

After several visits to the social work department, my parents agree it will be best if my baby brother gets placed into temporary foster care. With my mother in the hospital, my father can't manage everything on his own.

After a few more months passing and my baby brother now in local foster care, there is less stress on the family at home. However, my mother is still in a psychiatric hospital with little to no improvement. Due to my mother's mindset, the doctors want to try electric shock therapy; they suggest it is the best treatment for her. My mother's family and my sister decided to fight against the shock treatment, as they deemed it barbaric. After much persuasion, my father finally agrees with my mother's family and my sister, so the doctors get told not to use electric therapy.

Over a year has passed, and after more tests and discussions, the doctors diagnosed my mother with manic depression. They start giving her medication to balance her mood; she will take some tablets in the morning to perk her up, then some in the evening to bring her down. My father talks with the doctors and tells them he feels that my mother's new medication is working, so is there any chance that she can return home. The doctors agree that the drugs have made a significant difference and allow my father to sign her out and take her home.

However, my baby brother is not allowed to return home; he will remain with the foster family, allowing my mother time to recover fully.

When my mother gets home from the hospital, the medication given to her to help manage the depression has changed her; she is no longer acting like herself. My father now ultimately ruled the house; all terms that my mother had made for him to move back, no longer mattered. She is a shell of her former self and has no fight left in her. Most days, my mother will go to visit my brother and his foster carer Senga, they sit and talk for hours, my mother can open up to her. Senga is an asset to my family and my mother, and she plays a massive part in helping my mother get well. Senga is providing her with an escape away from our house and my father.

It is great having my mother back home; however, it doesn't change my father he is still abusive, nor does it stop the bullying from the kids in the street. Now I have reached puberty, and I'm baffled about my sexuality. Due to the stress in my life, psoriasis has appeared on my head, it's itchy and disgusting, and I have no self-esteem. I stop going to the hairdressers, and I wear white to camouflage the flakes of dandruff falling on my shoulders; I am living a nightmare.

Then one night as I am coming home from the shop, I get to the alley and notice Rab and Daz are there. I try not to look at them and go to walk around them, Rab steps in front of me preventing me from passing, so I ask him, what is it Rab what do you want? Rab says I don't want anything, and we are just being friendly and wondering what you are doing tonight? I answer, nothing, I am waiting in my house. Daz asks would you fancy hanging out and about with Rab and me, I'm confused why they would want to hang with me, but as I have no friends, I say, yes ok. Daz starts to laugh, then he says, that's cool we will come to get you about six.

I go straight home, I'm nervous and paranoid about what's just happened, I'm not sure if they are joking with me, or if they are planning to do something nasty, maybe they do want to hang with me. As I have not made any new friends since moving into my mother's; I think this could be my chance.

That night at six o'clock, there is a chap at the front door. It is Rab and Daz; I did not know what to do, so I just go out with them; at first, I'm nervous, and on edge, I watch every move they make. Rab can see I'm uncomfortable and tells me to chill out; they are not going to do anything.

Once I've relaxed, we have a crazy night which took my mind off everything, we start by stealing the apples from the tree in a neighbour's garden, then we egged some windows. We finish the night off by climbing onto the school roof, only to be chased by the janitor; we get up to no good, but I have a fantastic night with them.

I start to hang with Rab and Daz regularly; we get up to all sorts of mischief, going up to the woods all the time to build fires, I'm a pure firebug. When I am out with Rab and Daz, we just have great fun and never do any real harm.

One night I return home, my father can smell the smoke on my clothes. He asks me, have you been setting fires? I am too scared to tell a lie, so I admit to it.

My father gets so angry with me; however, he never beat me; he just tells me I am never again allowed out with Rab and Daz. He says, their crowd is nothing but trouble, don't you think this family has enough to deal with, without you bringing more problems to the door.

The next time I see Rab and Daz, I explain, my father has gone crazy at me for setting fires, and he has told me, I can no longer hang with you, they both say to me they are cool with it and thank me for not telling on them. However, if I see Rab or Daz in the alley, I stop and chat with them, it's good knowing they are my friends; now I only have to cope with the posh kids and Jake.

I am now fourteen years old, and in my second year of high school, my father has not sexually abused me for about two years, or since the court case with Peg Leg. I'm sleeping in my bed when I'm awoken by something touching my inner leg, I just lay there, I don't open my eyes, and I don't move. I know it is my father; after all this time, he has broken his promise, he told me he would never touch me again.

He starts to touch me, threw my boxers; he is kneeling by my bedside. He stops for a minute and plays with himself, then slips his hand back under my covers and starts touching me again. He gently lifts my blankets off my body then gently pulls down my boxers to expose my privates, I just lay there so still, pretending to be asleep.

He continues to touch me, and he is masturbating himself. Every so often, he will stop and be still; I think he is listening to be sure no one can hear him. My mother's house is much smaller than the old house, and It is easy for him to get caught. I thought this was all over, yet here he is again touching me, I feel ashamed of myself for just lying there, I never moved a muscle, I just pretended to be asleep, I am too afraid; I just keep thinking to myself, please stop, please go away, make this all be over. Eventually, my father finished masturbating himself, and he gets up from my bedside and leaves my room. I don't sleep that night; I have the fear he will come back and do it again.

The next morning, I can't even look at him, and he makes me feel sick. He again acts like he has done nothing wrong and says, make sure you wash today, that fucking psoriasis shit is flaking off you. It's fucking disgusting, so scrub yourself.

I am his fourteen-year-old son, and he just carries on like what he did is normal. At night every noise I hear, I think it's him coming for me, he has got me so afraid with nerves, and I don't sleep for three solid nights. I have to do something to make sure I am safe, so I ask my mother, can I get a lock for my door. She says, do you think I'm made of money, if you want a lock, you pay for it, so I start to look for a job to earn some cash to purchase a lock.

After a few weeks of looking, I get my first job; I am working on a paper run, I work seven mornings a week, earning sixty pounds every Friday. I start my papers every morning at five and finish at eight; then I would run and catch the bus to school from nine till four. It's hard work, and I don't want to use the bus because of Jake, but I want the money for my lock, so I put up with the bullying on the bus.

The first thing I purchase is the lock for my bedroom door; I asked my mother once again if she can buy me the lock; this time, I hand her a twenty-pound note. I tell her I want the lock because I am now a teenager and need some privacy.

That day when I return home, the lock is on my door and the key on my chest of drawers, I am so happy the first thing I do is slam the door shut and lock it. I do all the tests to make sure it is secure, and I feel safe; there is no way my father can get to me now.

Things are looking up, and thanks to the new lock on my door, I am now getting a decent knight sleep. My new job gives me spare cash every Friday, so I have started to buy new clothes and deodorant for myself.

My mother's medication is working, and she is slowly getting better, so my young brother can soon move out of Sengas foster care and back home.

CHAPTER SEVEN
Age 14 to 16

KAREN'S SECRET &
BEATING THE BULLIES

I'm sitting on the school bus on my way home, when Jake and his friends start mouthing off, as usual, they are laughing and pinging things at me. As the bus approaches my stop, I get up and go to the front; making sure to avoid them; I quickly get off, then I rush down the alleyway to my house.

As I enter the hallway, my mother shouts to me; you have a visitor, she is waiting in the kitchen. I walk into the kitchen, and Karen is sitting with this big smile on her face, she gets up cuddles me and says she has missed me. We both chat with my mother in the kitchen and then go through to my room.

The moment I closed my room door, Karen breaks down into tears, she slowly starts to tell me about her father. Karen says her father has sexually abused her for years, and she never told a soul. Recently the burden became too much, and Karen opened up and told her family everything. She says that her family do not believe her and that her mother called her a liar to her face, then her mother told her, she was no longer welcome in the family home and asked her to leave.

Karen tells me that because she spoke out against her father, he too got asked to leave the family home. With the police and social work getting involved, her mother is no longer allowed to foster children. Karen says her mother is outraged at the allegations she has made and blamed her for everything. Karen says her family is now in tatters, and it's all her fault for opening her big mouth.

I try to explain to Karen, she has done the right thing by speaking out, and her father should not be allowed to get away with it. Karen then gets so upset and says to me; even the police don't believe me, they told me there is insufficient evidence to charge him, and he is a free man. Callum no one believes me, and my parents are now getting a divorce, and none of my family wants to talk with me.

Feeling uncomfortable talking about sexual abuse in my house, I say to Karen; let's get out of here and go a walk to clear our heads. We walk to the shop to get something to eat, then continue to the park. Karen just keeps going over everything that her father did to her on the way to the park. I tell her it's horrific and that I can't believe he has gotten away with it.

In a few months, Karen will be turning sixteen and is heartbroken that her family have stopped talking with her, and devastated that they blame her for everything. As Karen has no other family, she gets forced to live in group accommodation for youths with challenging behaviours. Karen's life has turned completely upside down in a matter of days, and it's all because she spoke out. I want to tell her that my father is doing the same things to me, and I understand what she is going through. However, I can't do it, not now, and not after what she just told me about her family not believing her, and getting ripped apart.

I now know that I have to keep my secret forever; I can't tell anyone, not even my closest friend about what my father is doing to me. What if I did speak out and my family didn't believe me, and I don't want to be responsible for the destruction of my family. I think to myself; I'm not taking the risk of everything getting turned upside down, and then no one believes me.

As it starts to get late Karen tells me she has to go, as the unit where she is living has a curfew, and she has to be in for a set time each night.

As we walk to the bus stop, I notice the posh kids standing in a crowd next to the bus stop, I act normal and pretend not to see them. Jake doesn't appear to be with them, so I think perhaps they won't say anything, and Karen doesn't know the posh kids, and they don't know her.

As we approach the bus stop, they all start giggling and pointing over at us. Karen asks me, do you see that bunch of idiots and have they got a problem with us, why do they keep pointing over here and sniggering. I explain about them and tell Karen about Jake saying they are always nasty, and I ask that she just ignore them. Karen being Karen, can't do it, walks up to them and goes mental. Karen is swearing and screaming at them, whom the fuck does you guys think you are, do you think something is funny, do you think it's cool to bully people, do you want to see something that's funny? I will show you all a fucking joke as she squares up to them and gets right in their faces. Not one of them answer her back; they all back down and quickly walk away. It is not long before the bus arrives and as Karen gets on, she turns to me and says, Callum, please don't take that shit, you need to stand up to them, you are better than that and don't need to take it.

A few months pass, and I have not heard from Karen, I start to get worried, so I phone the accommodation where she is living. The woman on the other end of the phone informs me that Karen has moved on; she is no longer living with them. The woman tells me, as I am not a member of Karen's family, she will not disclose any further information and ends the call. Karen has just vanished into thin air, and after a few months of trying to find her, with no luck, I finally give up.

My attention slowly comes away from Karen, and it turns more toward this new family that has begun to move into our street. They are private and somewhat strange, only moving their belongings in during the night, and never during the day. Their curtains never get opened, and no one ever sees them.

One day as I'm passing the new neighbours house, I notice this young girl standing in the doorway, she is about my age. I'm intrigued by her family with them being so strange, so I decide to say hello. In the blink of an eye, this older woman comes running out the door and ushers the girl into the house. The older woman is all dressed in black with long white hair, she points toward me and shouts, you there, she doesn't want to talk with you, now go away, get out of here and don't bother us again. I stand there with my jaw dropped; I can't stop staring at her, as the old ladies' hand is all twisted and looks like it's melting; she keeps waving it at me and telling me to go away. As she turns her head to one side, her face is disfigured and also looks melted; she shrieks again, I know your types game, now I won't tell you again get out of here, she then goes in and slams her door.

A few days later, my mother comes home from the shop and tells me she was talking to the new family. I ask my mother, have you seen the state of the old ladies' face; I think she is a real-life witch. My mother says, don't you dare say those horrible things, I have been talking with her in the shop, and she is a nice lady, and she has invited me along tonight for a cup of tea and a chat. My mother then asks, would you like to come along, and you can see for yourself.

I decide to visit her with my mother, and I'm saddened to discover the truth, the old lady had almost died in a fire while saving someone's life. Her reason for moving to a new house was because the kids in the neighbourhood vandalized her property, and would shout names at her. They bullied her daughter because she has learning difficulties, and is different from them; resulting in her daughter not leaving the house to go out and play. The bullies had caused so much stress to her family; that's why she decided to move during the night; they never wanted anyone to see them and cause trouble.

The old lady is Gretta, and her daughter is Selena. I tell Gretta I'm sorry for approaching her daughter that day, and that I meant no harm, and that I was just trying to be friendly. Now knowing what they have gone through, I feel terrible for saying she was an old witch.

That night my mother and Gretta sit and discuss, Selena and Steves disabilities and all the clubs that my brother and Selena can attend. They also chat about all the disability benefits that each of them should be entitled to receive and any care components that they should also be getting.

It would appear our families have found common ground, and we all become good friends, it's not long before we are in and out of each other's houses. Gretta gradually allows Selena to come out and play on the street with me. Like me, Selena never got accepted into the posh gang, and I think it is because she has learning difficulties. I teach Selena to do normal things, like catching a ball or skipping; it takes Selena a long time to learn to do it by herself.

Selena has an older brother, his name is Peter, and he is in his early twenties, he is a bit of a loner, and over time, he and my sister become close.

My sister is spending more time with Gretta and her son, they go to church every Sunday, and my sister will go along. As time progresses, my sister becomes more and more distant from our family and then starts dating Peter.

A few times the police have come to Gretta's, concerned my mother asks if everything is ok. Gretta gets upset and tells my mother; it is all about the bullies from the old house, and there is an ongoing matter that the police are trying to clear up. There is no reason for Gretta to lie, so everyone believes her story and continues as usual.

Over time, small things don't add up with Gretta and her family, and my sister had let slip that their church is different from typical churches. She said everyone dresses in black, at times they chant in a strange language, they have a room for worship, and only a select few can enter.

More and more people on the street are telling my mother stories, saying Gretta worships the devil, and the church she visits is a cult. Worried my mother tells my sister to stop going to the church and asks that Gretta stops taking her. However, against my mother's wishes, Gretta sneaks my sister to her church.

That night while Gretta is out, a group of people turn up at Gretta's home and kick in her front door. They say they are looking for their daughter, before leaving they smash all her windows and paint a notice on her door saying, we found you, and we want our daughter back.

Because of what happened, my parents find out that Gretta has lied to them, and she has taken my sister to their so-called church. That same night they discover that my sister and Peter are in a relationship, and Gretta has known this for quite some time and has hidden it from them.

My family decided to keep away from Gretta, and my father is insistent that my sister has no contact with Peter. My sister gets upset, and she starts to turn against our family; she is fighting and arguing with my parents every day.

After about a week of them not seeing each other, Peter turns up at our front door, demanding to see my sister. Peter and my father get into a physical fight, and Peter gets the upper hand. During the commotion, my sister runs out of the house and leaves with Peter. When my parents asked Gretta, she denies knowing their whereabouts. She says she wants nothing to do with it, telling my parents if they don't believe her, they can come into her house and check for themselves that my sister is not in there.

A few days later, and yet again Gretta has done a moonlight flit, their house is empty, and my sister has gone.

My mother is frantic with worry and contacts the police, telling them about the Peg Leg court case and that my sister has money in the bank as compensation. She is worried that Gretta and Peter might be in a cult and after her cash.

When the police get back to my mother, it's not good news.

They tell my mother your daughter is almost sixteen years old; she is refusing to return home and wishes to stay with Gretta. The police tell my mother because of Beth's age; there is not a lot they can do. My mother is furious and says to them, well at this moment in time; she is still a minor, so I want my daughter brought home.

When the police return to collect my sister, she has gone, they manage to track Peter to a place of worship in the countryside. They struggle to get any information on my sister's whereabouts from the cult, and peter gives them no information at all. Knowing my sister will soon be sixteen, they show very little interest and don't pursue the matter.

While my sister is away from home, Peter becomes very abusive towards her; beating her, and forcing her to do things against her will.

When my sister's compensation money has run done, Gretta contacts the police to tell them where my sister can get located. She explains to the police, my sister had run away from home and asks they come to collect her.

When the police arrive and talk with my sister, she refused point-blank to return home and tells the police, she would rather die than come back and live in that house. The officers get the social work department involved, and the social workers give my sister the option, go home, or go into care. My sister, not willing to return home, chooses to go into childcare and ends up placed at a children's home.

Now the family knows where my sister is living, my parents regularly visit, trying to persuade her to return home, my sister always refuses.

I continually ask my parents, can I visit my sister, and when will she come home. The answer is always the same; it is your sister's choice to be there, so no, you can't go and visit her.

Then one random day my mother asks me, would you like to go

and visit your sister, I say yes, and can't wait to go and see her.

As we arrived, I am taken back by the home's beauty; it is a splendid big castle on a hill, with views for miles, I can see my sister standing by the doors of the home, and I feel so good to see her. While my parents spoke with the people in charge, my sister and I explored the grounds. They are marvellous; there is walled gardens, vineyards, and all sorts of plants and trees; it is just like a fairy-tale land, and every turn has something new to explore.

As we walk through the grounds talking, I keep trying to persuade her to come home. She tells me sorry for leaving, but there is no way she can return, and I of all people should understand why.

My Sister did everything when my mother was in the hospital, and my father was also cruel to her. I can't blame her for not wanting to return home, there are no good memories, and no reason to return, and I wouldn't want to either.

Time passes so fast that day, and it is hard to say goodbye, I loved seeing her, and we have such a close bond with each other. Before I leave, I tell her that I miss her and just want her to come home.

That day when we arrive home, my mother is on the phone non-stop, she is persistent and trying to get my sister to return home.

With my sister in the children's home, and not there to protect me, I feel more alone and vulnerable than ever. My father is getting angry at the smallest of things, and my psoriasis has become much worse, covering eighty per cent of my body. It's dry and itchy, I scratch at it continually, and I know it's disgusting. Still, the itch is just too intense, and I can't resist, and my scratching is making my father get agitated. He starts to become paranoid and keeps telling me to stay away from him with my flaky skin, and that he doesn't want to catch that filth from me.

I'm standing in the doorway of the kitchen, there is food on the kitchen table, and I start scratching at my arm, some of my skin flakes off and lands on the floor. My father can see this from the living room, and it infuriates him. He gets up and stomps past me into the kitchen, picks all the plates up from the table, and one by one dumps them into the bin. He starts shouting; we don't want to catch that filth from you, you have contaminated the food with that fucking disease, you're fucking disgusting, now get to fuck out of the kitchen.

He pushes me from the kitchen doorway, making me fall back and landing on the floor of the hall, he then drags me into my bedroom and beats me. While beating me, he is shouting; it's all your fault, no one will get dinner, from now on when food is cooking, you will not go near that kitchen, do you understand me? If I catch you near that kitchen, I will kick the shit out of you, and I will do it again and again until it penetrates that thick skull.

My father starts to remind me daily, just how disgusting he finds my flaky skin, and how I should never go near the kitchen. He tells me when food is getting cooked, I am not allowed to come out of my room, and my bedroom door must get closed. With my father continually bombarding me with insults, I start to grow a complex and try to cut my scaly patches off with a razor blade. Cutting my skin doesn't help and makes things worse. I have to stop participating in school sports as I don't want the other kids to see my skin, so I deliberately forget my gym gear. The teachers at school are giving me a hard time, lecturing me because I never take part, so they punish me by making me write essays.

I'm ashamed and embarrassed with my body and start wearing big jumpers and jeans, I even wear them during the hot summers, as it's the only way to hide my skin. I've become very depressed, and every night I'm crying myself to sleep, I just feel so alone and wish my life to be different.

There is one good thing, now that I have my new lock on my bedroom door, I'm safe from my father, he thinks my skin is disgusting and contagious anyway, so there is no way he will want to touch me. Even if he wanted to, he can't get into my room because of my new lock, and for once, I can get a decent knight sleep and feel safe.

I soon realise I'm wrong when I'm sleeping in my bed, and once again awoken to feel this sensation on my privates. It is my father, and he is on his knees by my bedside, his head is under my covers, and he is licking my privates then he starts to suck me. I am so scared, and I don't know what to do, I'm just lying there fully paralysed in fear. I'm thinking, how could he have possibly got into my room, I have the new lock, and I made sure the door was locked, I even got back out of bed to recheck, there is no way I left that door unlocked.

As I lay there, I have this idea; I will pretend to wake up and hopefully; this will make him go away. First, I moved a little and made a groaning noise, hoping he will stop. He just continues, so then I thought if I wake up and I talk loud enough, someone will hear me and wake up, and If he thinks someone else is awake, he may not take the risk and leave me alone.

I lay still for a minute, working up the courage, I then do it, I sit right up and say to him, loudly, what are you doing to me, leave me alone.

My father quickly covers my mouth with his hand, hushing me, and whispering it's all right Callum, I have got a spare key, and I have locked the door, so we can't be disturbed. He then pushes my head back down onto the pillow, whispering into my ear, now you be quiet Callum, as he slowly removes his hand from my mouth. I'm terrified, and I just lay there staring at the top bunk, pretending to be somewhere else. He continues to suck me and masturbate me until I ejaculated, my father then licked the cum from me and masturbated himself. I hate myself and my life, I'm sick to my stomach, and I feel helpless and ashamed of what's happening, and now he has a key to lock the door from the inside of the room.

The next day I am feeling so low and dirty, I just want it all to end, I have no way to make him stop. I decide the best thing to do is take my own life, so I go into the kitchen and take the box of paracetamol, some other tablets, and half a bottle of vodka. I walk around the streets thinking about everything, and I start to swallow one pill after another as I swig at the vodka; I can no longer go on like this. I just want it all to end, and my life to be over, I keep thinking about him touching me, and the smell of him, it is disgusting, and I feel so alone. I walk to the local bridge with the intentions of throwing myself into the river. I have now become drowsy due to the tablets and vodka, and everything becomes foggy. I attempt to climb over the bridge to jump, but I fall back and land on the footpath.

Laid out on the ground crying, and it is such a cold evening, I'm shouting at the thin air and thinking I'm talking to God. I'm saying, What the fuck have I done to deserve this life, why are you doing this to me? I start to scream and punch myself on the head, wanting to hurt myself. Suddenly this calmness comes over me, and I think back to the good old times with my Grandfather Jim and Papa Mack. Papa Mack had taken me on a trip to Oban, and there was only one space left on the bus, and he chose me out of all the other grandkids. I'm thinking back to that moment and feel loved and wanted. I must have passed out at that point; as I can't remember very much else.

The next morning, I awake to feel this little old lady nudging me with her walking stick; she is asking if I am ok, and her little dog is licking my face. She must have thought I was crazy; I just looked at my watch, jumped up and said, I'm late for my paper run, then I ran off away from her.

That day I slowly walk around my papers; I feel like I have my grandparents by my side. As I walk, I have so many things racing through my mind, and for every disturbing thought, I have a good memory, it is like I am being pushed past the bad times by my grandparents. I think to myself, I,m not taking this any-more, I've had enough, and decide to do something to change it. I start saving all the money from my paper run, then I purchase a multi-gym for my bedroom and start working out every day. I need to fix my problems; no one is coming to my rescue; it is down to me.

I'm just a skinny wee thing, no muscle, only skin and bone. Still, I have to start somewhere, so I purchase the latest protein shakes, and become determined and dedicated to being strong enough to take on my father, and the bullies. I plan to sort out all the bullies first, then when I am strong enough, I will beat the crap out of my father. I'm going to make sure he can't hurt me or anyone ever again; I will be the one to stop him.

I have been working out for several months now, then one night as I am walking along the street, I can see Jake. Jake starts all his usual bullying tactics, and his full gang of friends appear to be with him. With all his friends there it just makes Jake worse; they encourage him by laughing and pushing him to say and do more, Jake loves to show off in front of them; he likes having the audience.

It all starts with Jake saying look guys; it's the wee poof, and what's that stink, that's right it's just Callum, he stinks of shite because he likes to jobby jab. Just like clockwork, they all laugh at me, I just ignore his comments and keep walking. Then he says what's up can't you hear me, are you deaf, oh that's right, I forgot, you're just like your little mongo brother, deaf and dumb, and once again they all start laughing.

I go into a red rage; I can't see anything but his face; I just run at him and start punching him over and over on his face. I can't control myself, and he is pleading for me to stop. All his friends scamper like little rats; there not laughing now. Jake is trying to get away from me, and as he turns to run, I grab his head from be-hind and push my fingers into his eye sockets. I start biting into the back of his head over and over; I am like a wild animal. Eventually, his mother and other parents come running to his rescue, and as they try to prise my hands off of his face, I dig my nails in all the more.

Finally, they get me off of him, and as he turns to face me, I can see the damage I have inflicted. Jake's nose got burst wide; his face has deep scratches, anyone would think a wild cat had mauled him, both his eyes are bloodshot red and blackened, and the back of his neck and head covered in bloody bite marks.

I was like a crazed beast, and the whole time he was pleading for me to stop; however, I could not control myself. Eventually, everyone was out in the street due to the disturbance, including my mother and Jake's mother. I still had so much rage, I could feel it inside me, I wanted to kill him.

When everything calmed down, Jake's mother asks my mother to look at her son's face. Then she says to my mother, your son is an animal, it's not discipline he needs, it's putting down. My mother looked at her and said, very calmly, I think your son had this coming to him for a long time now, and I don't think he is the innocent party in all this, do you? My mother knew I had put up with a lot from Jake and his gang of bullies, so she never gave me into trouble for what I did to him. Instead, my mother just hugged me and told me she is proud of me, and well done for standing up to the bullies.

A few weeks pass since the fight with Jake, and things have changed, I have become mister popular, and all of his so-called friends wanted to be friends with me, they had all just dumped Jake and treated him like he was never their friend.

After that day, none of them ever laughed at me; I think they all knew I would no longer take it. Then I start to become friends with all the posh kids, including Jake. It's a relief knowing that I don't have to worry about all the kids in the street, including Rab and Daz; I can go to the shop or come home from school without being on edge.

One day, my mother has gone out, and I am sitting in the living room on the floor, I am sat in front of the TV when my father walked in and closed the Living room door with a bang. I get a fright and instantly know he is up to something; I start to get very nervous and stand up to leave the room. I just kept looking at the TV and thinking I need to get out of here, so I glance around at him, he is standing in front of the door and blocking my exit.

Then he said why do you keep looking at me, is it a crime to stand in my living room. My father then moves closer and is positioned directly behind me; I just want to get out of there.

I start to walk around him, and as I go to open the door, he places his foot in front of it, preventing the door from opening, he steps in front of me and asks are you going somewhere? I look at him with fear, stuttering I say, yes dad, I am just going out with my friends. Then pointing across the living room, he said not without picking up that, as he pointed to my cereal bowl. I have this sudden feeling of relief come over me, I think to myself thank god it's just my bowl. I quickly turn around to pick up my cereal bowl, and he grabs me from behind, he bear-hugs me and starts to squeeze me so tight, and then he throws me onto the sofa. I quickly get to my feet and face him, he pushes me back down on to the sofa and says, do you think you are hard enough? He starts to laugh at me, and I try again to go around him and leave the room, he pulls me back in.

I began to scuffle with him, I'm trying to get away, and he pulls my T-shirt over my head and throws it on to the floor. He pulls me into a headlock, rubbing his knuckles onto my head and mocked me for not being able to fight back. Once he finished mocking me, he lets me go then pushes me back onto the sofa. I try so hard to get away; however, he is just too strong for me. He climbs on top of me, sits on my stomach using his knees to stop my arms from moving; he has me pinned, and I can't move; He is on top of me and mocking me. He does this thing called the typewriter on my chest, poking me with his fingers and laughing; it's not sore but is very irritating. I struggle to get up, but I just can't he is too heavy for me, then he grabs at my nipples and starts to twist them. I am yelling at him to get off me and leave me alone, it just makes him do it all the more, he is laughing, and shouting in my face, I know you like it and keeps twisting my nipples. I began to wriggle about trying to get myself free, but he slaps me on the face and is just too strong for me. My father then put one hand round my throat and began to strangle me; I can't breathe, and with his knees still pinning my arms, I can't move. He puts his second arm around his back and down my jogging pants, he starts grabbing at my penis and genitals, he is pulling on them with one hand and choking me with the other. He lets my privates go as I almost get free, then he pinned me again. He puts his hand back down my joggers several times and is playing with me; then he grabs hold of them and twisted. The pain is excruciating, and I just keep screaming at him, get off me, get fucking off me, I hate you, I fucking hate you.

Then as quick as it all started, it stops, he stands up picks up my T-shirt, flings it at me, and tells me, fuck off, get out of here, you're a fucking little sissy, just get out of my sight.

I ran for the front door and got out, then ran until I could not breathe anymore. I began to walk along the shore until I came to a little beach area. I sit there on that small beach for hours and hours, and I am going over in my head how I can get rid of him, I consider killing him at one point, I think I could do it as he sleeps. It starts to get cold and dark, the midges are biting me all over, so I headed home, knowing my mother will be back.

When I arrive home, my mother asks, where have you been all day, I just reply, out with friends, then I go straight into my room and close the door.

Weeks go past, and all the time my father is growling at me, each time I walk past him, he flinches his arm and pretends he is going to punch me. I am so nervous around him, I jump at his every move, scared to leave my room even to use the toilet, I just hide in there most days.

Then at night as I am sleeping, he sneaked into my room again and punched me right in the stomach as I slept, catching me off guard. I am gasping for air, and he grips my nose and my mouth, covering it with his hand and preventing me from breathing. As my father is pushing my head into the pillow, he put his face against mine and whispers in my ear; this is just a reminder Callum I can get to you anytime I like. He then calmly walks out of my room, locking the door behind him and returning to the living room to play his computer. It is a nightmare, I'm already struggling to sleep at night, and this just makes things worse, he has punched me in the guts several times now as I lay sleeping. It is living torture, and I am terrified to sleep.

About four months have gone past, and every day my father is mocking me and bullying me, pretending he is going to hit me. He never once lets up, then randomly on this morning, my father is super nice to me; his behaviour is making me feel uncomfortable.

Since the fight with Jake, the posh kids have been coming to my door and asking me if I want to hang with them. On this day, the posh kids come to the front door, and my father answers, however, before allowing me to go to the door, he tells me to go through to the kitchen. He then asks me, Callum, would you like to invite all your friends into your room today, I can't believe what I'm hearing, so I ask him again; just to be sure. He replies, your friends can come into your room, that's if you want. I am so excited and thank him; however, I did find it odd as my father never let us bring anyone into the house.

I then thought he has been kind to me all morning; perhaps he is just having a good day; besides, it's not like he would try anything, not in front of all my friends.

I go back outside and invited everyone into my room; the

weather outside was not great, so everyone is happy to be inside. After sitting in my room for about five minutes, we all decided to watch a movie, so we pooled our cash together, went to the shop, and bought loads of sweets, crisps and juice.

It's fantastic; all my friends get comfy, we put the movie on and started to share out all our treats. About fifteen minutes pass, and we are snacking and enjoying the film, and I feel amazing. I can't believe I have all these friends, I never had friends in my bedroom before, watching movies, and sharing sweets with me. Just at that point, my bedroom door bursts open, it's my father, he starts hurling all this abuse at me saying, do you think this is a fucking doss house, and did I tell you to invite the whole street in here. Are you deliberately trying to take the cunt out of me, do you think this is a fucking hotel or something? Now, get your friends to fuck out of my house, and you're grounded. Then he turns to all my friends and roars at them, well, what are you all waiting for, did you lot not hear me? I said, get out.

All my friends are shocked by his actions, and they put their shoes on and get out the door quick as lightning. I just kept apologizing to them; it is so embarrassing.

I have no idea why my father did that to me; it is just nasty. Usually, there would be a reason, perhaps, he lost on his computer, or because I went into the kitchen with my flaky skin. This time there is no reasoning for his behaviour; it is just random, and he appeared to be in a perfectly good mood beforehand.

After the movie day, my friends ask me, why is your father always so mean to you? Why is he such a dick? I always change the subject; I make an exception with my friend Dianne. I tell her all the things he did to my sister and me, always careful not to mention the sexual abuse. I can't open up about that; I am too scared of all the bad things my father had said would happen. After all, Karen had spoken out about her father sexually abusing her, and he got away with it, and it destroyed her family for nothing. Then there was Peg Leg, he has pleaded guilty to twelve accounts of child abuse in a court to a judge, and he still walks free. I even tried turning to my school; I told them it was happening and look where that got me, my father managed to completely twist it, making me out to be the liar. Many things stopped me from talking, my sister being away from home, my mother having a breakdown, and most of all, the manipulations and fear from my father.

My friend Dianne is great to talk with; however, Dianne could never replace my sister. My sister and I have been through so much together, and she is the only person who understands just how evil my father can be.

I am ecstatic when I hear the news; my mother has received a phone call; it is from the children's home, and my sister has decided she will return home and live with us. I think that's why my parents let me visit her; they knew if she saw me, it would prompt her to come home.

My sister does not return home straight away; there is lots of meetings, documents and paperwork that my parents have to complete first.

It has been a few weeks now, and my sister has returned home, she did not tell me the reason for coming back; I believe it is for me. She never speaks about what happened with Peter or when she was in that cult. What I do know is that he was not pleasant to her, and made her do things she did not want to do. I never asked her about what has happened; I just know she never wanted to talk about it.

With my sister being home, things are very different in the house. It is almost like my father is scared of her. Usually, when my father asks for a task to get done everyone jumps, and it gets done. However, when my sister returned from the children's home, she rebelled against him, she answers him back and tells him, it's not my mess, so I'm not cleaning it. When my father beat me, my sister would get in his way and shout at him, do you think that it makes you look hard, hitting on a little boy;

why don't you hit someone that can fight back. I'm not sure why my father never argued back with her, perhaps something happened at the children's home to make him think twice.

I am going into my fourth year of secondary school, and things are going well, it is not long after my fifteenth birthday when my sister meets this guy called CJ. CJ is a bit of a hard guy around town and is known for being a troublemaker. He is well known by the police and is from a rough area. My sister and CJ get on well together, and he is generous to her.

After a few months of them dating, my sister decided she wants a fresh start, so she decides it is time for her to move out. I am devastated, and don't want her to leave; however, I am happy for her at the same time. My sister has managed to keep my father at bay for the past year, and I started to think, what if he goes back to his old ways. With my sister gone, who will stop him?

As soon as I knew my sister was leaving, I began to work out on my multi-gym day and night; I am getting ready for my father, this time if he started, I will not be so submissive.

It took a few months before my sister got offered a flat, and it is a few more months before she moves out. My exams have started in school; I am worrying so much about life at home that I can't focus on anything. I get myself so stressed out, my psoriasis has flared up and is now covering eighty per cent of my body, it is all through my hair, on my body, arms and legs, it is so itchy. I am scratching at it so much that my skin has started to split and weep, luckily my hands and face are not affected, and I can hide it.

My friends and I have started drinking and taking recreational drugs over the weekends. I don't like drugs; I only take them to be part of the in-crowd. I have two groups of friends, the posh kids', that's the group I hang with on weeknights in our street, we don't do much, we sit around and chat or watch movies in each other's houses. The popular group of friends I hang with on the weekends, mostly going down to the town centre or up to the park getting up to mischief, drinking and trying different types of drugs.

Over the past couple of years, I got myself into several fights coming out on top. I think that's how the popular kids accepted me into their group, and I guess they respected me for standing up for myself. My sister also got into several fights over the past few years, beating the girls in a bad way. With my sister now dating CJ, the local bad boy, people knew we are not going to take the crap anymore. No one ever calls me a poof anymore; however, my closest friends still tease me and say, are you sure you're not gay, not even a little bit, or they will joke with me and ask me; do you think that guy over there looks hot?

One night on the weekend after being out with my friends, I come home to find my mother and father having a party. Everything is going well, and everyone appears to be enjoying themselves and having drinks and nibbles. However, after several hours of drinking and partying, most of the people decide to leave.

My aunt Gillian and her second husband Tam, wait behind, and the four of them choose to play a game of darts. The dartboard is in the hallway; it is a long narrow hall, with all the rooms of the house going off each side. My bedroom is the end door, right where they had all gathered to play darts. I can hear them all talking about adult stuff, and as the night goes on, they get louder.

As my father became more intoxicated, his pretence personality broke down, and his real nasty side starts to come out. My father begins to get nasty toward my mother, telling everyone, just how crap she is at darts, and she can keep her fat arse in the kitchen, as no one wants to see her flabby arse.

My aunt Gillian noticed my mother is getting upset by his comments, and she defended my mother and spoke up at my father. Ronald that is my sister you are talking to, don't you think you should lower your tone? Don't be so fucking cheeky to her; you seem to forget, she's the one that does everything for you and those kids. It might even help, if you started paying her a bit more dammed respect, instead of treating her like crap.

My father decides to play it cool; he tells my aunt he is only joking, then he apologises to them both.

After he apologised, everyone decided to move on from the argument, and the night seemed to be going well, everyone continued drinking and playing darts. However, the way my aunt has spoken to my father is eating away at him.

After a while, my father starts with all the sniping comments toward my aunt and her husband. He begins by saying to my uncle tam; you don't let her go out in a skirt like that, do you? If that were my woman, she wouldn't be wearing that; I like to keep my woman in line. He then starts bringing up her kids, saying to her; it must be hard Gillian knowing that your kids chose to stay with their real dad, and not to stay with you. The whole thing blew up fast, and tam says right, I've heard enough of this shit, we're not listening to his crap anymore, lets phone a taxi and go home.

As my aunt and uncle are leaving, my father makes one final comment, telling my aunt that her kids are better off with their real dad and away from her. Everything exploded, and I am standing in the doorway of my bedroom, watching the whole thing unfold.

My aunt makes a mad dash up the hallway at my father, a full-scale fight breaks out between them, she is punching and scratching at his face, and both of them are screaming at each other. My mother and Tam managed to get wedged between them and separate them. However, not before my aunt managed to get one final slap across my father's face, the slap is so loud. My father has scratches and a big red handprint all over his face from where my aunt had hit him. It was incredible seeing her attack him; he certainly deserved it.

My aunts' taxi had arrived, then left due to all the commotion, so my aunt phones for a second taxi, this time she and Tam wait outside for it. During this short wait, my father turns his aggression toward my mother. He starts to shout at her; your sister is a fucking cow, look what she did to my face, this is all your fault for inviting them. I don't want your cow of a sister back in my house, that cow is not welcome in here anymore, do you hear me? My mother gets angry and answers him back. She pipes up at him, that's the problem Ronald, this is not your house, it's my house, and if I want my sister in my home, she will be in my house, it is my name on that door, not yours.

My father completely loses it, he clenches his fists, throws his hands into the air, then lets out a mighty roar. My mother in a panic turns to run, he reaches out and tries to grab her, he chases her down the hallway. He swings a punch, catching her on the back of her head, then she stumbles forward and as she falls, smacks her head off of the radiator. My mother is just lying there on the ground; she is motionless. I start to scream, over and over I'm saying don't die, please mum, don't die, please get up.

My aunt Gillian burst back through the front door; she is shouting at my father, what the fuck have you done to my sister, what did you do to her. My mother then randomly jumps to her feet, she looks confused and covered in blood, she runs right out the front door and down the street. My aunt Gillian goes after her, and they get about two hundred yards when my mother collapses to the ground again, and she is just lying there. Within minutes, an ambulance has appeared, and they take my mother to the hospital. She spends the night in the hospital and never tells the doctors the truth, she says she had just fallen and bumped her head on the radiator. I think she convinced herself, that's what happened, and once again, my father has gotten away with it.

After the night of the fight, my mother is a different person, and she became very nervous around my father. Whatever my father said, she did without hesitation. If he told her to jump from a cliff, she would step off; there is no life or fight left in her, she hardly spoke and did what she got told to do by my father.

My mother's family decided to keep away and not talk to her, and they are angry because she sided with my father over them. My mother never had a choice, he is controlling her, and she is physically and mentally ill. My sister has no idea what is going on; she has her own house and is under the impression everything is ok at home. My father has managed to push my mother's family away, so he has complete control over everything.

A few months go by, and my mother's mental health sees no improvement, so she ended up in another psychiatric ward. This time it is a local hospital set up for people with mental health problems. The place is like a ray of sunshine for my mother, and instantly, we see an improvement in her mental health, and she has met lots of new friends. Most of them understood my mother's health issues, as they too are going through similar experience's in life. I think my mother suddenly knew that she is not alone, and there is support for her. One of the people she meets is a lady called Susan, Susan has many issues, and her way to deal with things is to self-harm.

After several months of my mother being in the Psychiatric ward, there is a massive improvement to her health. She is permitted to leave; however, she must attend a group session weekly. At the group session, my mother talks openly about things going on in her life, and her mind, everything is private within her group. The group sessions have a massive impact on my mother's road to recovery, and she also starts to get out of the house more often. My mother regularly goes to visit Senga, the woman who fostered my baby brother, Senga is also helping with my mother's recovery. My mother's family decide to put their differences to one side and start talking to her again.

I have now turned sixteen, and life over the past year has been a rollercoaster of emotions, I am still pushing myself on the multi-gym. My father has no time to bully me, with my mother going in and out of the hospital, and my sister getting her flat, he is far too busy dealing with my three young brothers. My brother Steve has become a right handful and gone into the kitchen and broken all the eggs on to the kitchen table, then poured the milk, flour, sugar and coffee on top of it. When my father walks into the kitchen, Steve is sitting there with a cake book open. He is mixing the contents on the table together, and I think he is trying to make my father a cake. I found it extremely cute and funny; however, my father did not find it amusing; of course, I got told to clean up the mess. Having my brothers keeping my father extremely busy gives me a break.

My final months of school are also approaching, which makes me extremely happy; I feel relief to be leaving school, as my time there was horrible. The teachers never gelled with me, and it was only in the past couple of years, I had made any real friends.

On this day, as I am approaching the school gates, I can see Karen stood there. I'm so excited as I have not seen her in years, I approach her expecting a big welcome. However, she is acting sluggish and distant. We get on to the bus, and I ask her if she has been drinking, Karen said nope, and started to giggle, she then said to me, in a sluggish tone, you are so silly, I just want to see my wee pal Callum.

During the bus journey home, I just kept staring at her; she is struggling to put sentences together.

When leaving the bus, Karen becomes extremely unbalanced on her feet and incoherent with her speech. Walking the short distance home, I have to prop her up and support her to walk, and upon reaching my front gate, Karen tells me she has taken some pills and drank some stuff from under her mother's kitchen sink. Just at this point, my aunt Morag has pulled up in her car; I tell my aunt, I think Karen has taken something, my aunt said, you're not kidding, and ask that I help put Karen into her car.

My aunt Morag drove Karen straight to the hospital, Karen gets her stomach pumped, and they keep her in for observation overnight.

When Karen gets out of the hospital, she seems different, and I only see her on a rare occasion. I ask what's going on with her, and she tells me she got made to see a psychiatrist, and our friendship starts to grow distant from that day.

A few months later, I find out that Karen is dating a guy and he has a flat, so that's where she has been hiding. I hear through friends that he has not been too kind to her, and one neighbour even said she had seen them fighting in the middle of the street, and they had both knocked lumps out of each other. The times that I did see Karen, she never spoke about her new man.

I blamed Karen's father for her mental state, because of the years he had sexually abused her; I think her life would have been very different had he not done that to her. Yet, her father walked free, just as Peg Leg did, and my father's brother bobby. There was no justice for their crimes.

Decision time has come, and I decide I will not stay on at school.

I have this one teacher, Miss M; she is horrible to me, and every day she will find a reason to pick on me. It's almost like she enjoys it, and she has this high-pitched tone that goes right through me.

Every day she will send me to the back of the dinner cue for no apparent reason, and She will say, look at me when I'm talking to you, and with her finger poke me right on my shoulder. Then she says is it any wonder you are the way you are, just look at you. Well, I can't say I'm surprised, you only have to look at your upbringing, and I can't imagine you will ever amount to any-thing. Oh, and Callum, can no one in your household work an iron? She is just horrible to me. One-time she pushed me so far; I flung a chair at her and got suspended. I put up with Miss M for four years, every day in that school she was there picking on me. Trying to deal with her and cope with everything at home, was just too much. Miss M and my father had both swayed my decision not to better my education, and because of them, I wanted to leave. I wanted out of school as soon as I possibly could; I wanted to get a job, work all day and all night, that way I could leave it all behind me, get a house and never see any of them again.

CHAPTER EIGHT

Age 16 to 20

HIS FINAL ACT &
MEETING SHELBY

Now out of school and only doing my paper run, things did not turn out how I expected, it is not as easy to get a job as I thought, I start to become a bit of a recluse. I do my paper run in the morning, go to the shop and buy a bottle of drink, then sit by myself in my locked bedroom. All-day long, I watch old tv soaps with a bottle and get drunk, then I listen to music until I pass out. I just want to block out all the horrible things and pretend everything is just fine.

I have been doing the same routine for about six months now, papers, get drunk, watch tv, go to sleep, I just keep drinking myself into my little world. Half the time, I don't even notice the people around me.

Then one night in the early hours, my father decides he is going to get up to his old tricks and take advantage of me. I drink a lot, and I am only sixteen, but I had matured over the past few years.

It is four o'clock in the morning, and I will be waking up for my paper run at five-thirty. I'm fast asleep and was drinking the night before. I awake to this sensation on my privates; it's my father he is kneeling at my bedside and masturbating himself while sucking on my penis.

As I lay there, I have many thoughts going through my mind; I do not move a single muscle, and while opening my eyes to stare at him, I calmly say in a clear and accurate tone. You are not getting any younger, soon you will be a frail old man that can't defend yourself, then I will hurt you, you will beg me to stop, but I will keep going, and there will be nothing you can do to stop me.

My father never said a word to me; he just stops what he is doing, stands up, pulls up his shorts and then walks out the door.

I quickly get out of bed, slam the room door and lock it, my whole body is shaking, I have to get out, I feel so trapped in my room, so I fling on my clothes and run out the door to do my papers.

I am about an hour too early for my run, and the shop keeper has not yet arrived to open.

I am standing there outside the shop a complete wreck; I can't believe I have stood up to my father and made him stop.

As I'm standing outside the shop waiting for it to open, it's a nightmare; I am on edge with every car that passes, thinking it's my father.

When the shop keeper finally arrives, he asked, have you been waiting here long, and is everything ok? I reply in a nervous tone; I can't sleep, and yes, I'm ok. The shop keeper has known me for a long time, and I know he can tell something is not right with me. I quickly gather my papers and leave the shop.

As I walk around my paper run, I am so proud of myself for what I said to my father, at the same time, I'm scared there will be consequences. My emotions are all over the place, and as I approach the end of my run; there is this little set of garages, and I can see my father's car, he has parked between them. I am so scared to walk past, my whole body starts to shake, and I feel sick with nerves; however, I know I have to be confident.

I start to walk toward the car, and as I pass, I look in through the windscreen directly at him, I keep my head held high, and I am so relieved as I go passed.

I hear his car engine start-up, and he slowly drives the car alongside me, rolling his window down, he says, Callum, can we talk please, I ignore him and keep walking. He asks, Callum please just get into the car, I only want to speak to you.

Taking all my courage, I stop walking and turn to look directly at him. I say with a shaky voice, I know what you have done to me is wrong, and I'm not letting you do it anymore, I'm going to tell my mother.

My father starts pleading with me, please stop and think about what you are doing, listen to me, please, just stop for a minute and listen. I admit it was wrong of me, I wish I never did it to you, and I don't know why I did. My father then started crying and says, it's too late to change what I've done to you, and I can only say, I'm sorry, I promise you it will never happen again.

I shake my head at him, and say, I've heard all of this before, you are a liar, and then I walk away.

My father continues to follow me in his car, and still crying, he starts telling me about his childhood. He explained, how his brother Bobby had raped him over and over as a child and then had beat him, he said he told people, and no one listened to him.

My father then starts sobbing uncontrollably, and he keeps saying, I'm sorry Callum, please I'm sorry for what I've done. I swear to you, I will never hurt you again, please I promise you. Over and over, he asks me not to say anything to my mother.

I don't listen to his false promise, then he says Callum; please, it will tear our family apart, and your mother will be broken-hearted. When she finds out what has happened, she won't be able to cope and will go back to that hospital, and they will take your brothers away from her, and your brothers will get dumped into care. Please, Callum, I'm not lying to you, I promise you, that's what will happen if you tell anyone.

In that instant, I thought about Karen, she had ended up in a unit for kids, and her family got torn apart, I did not want that for my brothers. What if my mother did take a breakdown and ended back in the hospital; It would all be my fault.

I tell my father; I will not say anything as long as you never touch me again, but it's not for you that I keep it secret it's for my mother.

My father thanks me, then promised me that he would never hurt or sexually abuse me again. I ask him just to go away and leave me alone, so he drove off.

As soon as his car is out of range, I go into complete pieces, I sit down on the pavement against the fence, and cry to myself. I know I'm letting him away with it, but there is nothing I can do, not without hurting everyone else, I feel so trapped.

After completing my paper run, I return home, and my father is extremely nervous around me. His behaviour reminded me of how he acted when my sister first returned from the Children's Home.

Not long after confronting my father, a woman named Susan, and her daughter Lisa came to visit my mother. My mother had met Susan during her time at the psychiatric ward, and both of them became good friends. Susan's daughter, Lisa, is such a beautiful looking girl, and we both find that we have a lot in common with each other, and we instantly click. Lisa's parents are going through a divorce, her Grandparents both passed away with cancer, and her mother was in and out of the psychiatric hospital.

Lisa and her mother start to visit regularly, and the more people that see Lisa and me together begin to assume we are a couple. Then her mother says, don't you two think you would make a lovely couple, you would probably both be better off as a couple as your always together. Both of us just smiled, then laughed at one another.

Lisa had several boyfriends during our friendship, and she is not shy with the boys. I have never had a proper girlfriend, and I am still a virgin, and my friends have started to pressure me into getting a girlfriend, and asking if I'm gay. I'm confused about my sexuality and unsure of what I want, I still feel attracted to guys, and even though I don't want to feel this way, I can't control it. I don't tell anyone, and I continue to fight against my inner emotions. I blame my thoughts for being gay on the sexual abuse done to me, and I'm disgusted by myself.

One day we are all sitting in my mother's kitchen, and Susan boiled the kettle then got some cups out to make tea, once the kettle has boiled, she picks it up and without warning pours the scalding hot water all down herself. I can't believe what I'm seeing, and everyone rushes around to help her. After an hour or so, everything calms down, and Lisa and I decide to go for a walk.

We chatted about everything and opened up to each other, talking about our mother's mental health's, and how it has put so much pressure on our families. Lisa and I kissed that night, and we decided to start going out together as a couple. It's a good feeling, and I dismiss the fact that I'm still confused with my sexuality.

A few months pass, and everything is going well between us. Lisa then drops a bombshell; she discovers she is pregnant, and the child is her ex-boyfriends. We talk about it, and she completely understands If I don't want to see her anymore. Life is good for us, and both our families get on well together, so I tell her I want to stand by her, and we continue as a couple. We both start looking at baby stuff, everything is moving so fast, and we are both still living with our parents.

Things are starting to look up, a few months pass, and my father has backed entirely off and left me alone. I am happy and more confident in myself, perhaps I am not gay after all, and it is just a phase I'm going through. Then Lisa hits me with the bad news, she has lost the baby and will still have to give birth; It is devastating. After the birth of the child, Lisa's family decide to hold a funeral, and afterwards, the wake would take place at her aunt's house. The whole experience is heart-breaking for everyone.

At the wake, Lisa disappeared from the crowd; I presumed she wants to get some space.

As Lisa has gone for some time, I become concerned and decide to go and look for her. I'm walking up the stairs, and hear noises coming from the spare bedroom, I slowly opened the door, and there is Lisa in bed with her ex-boyfriend, both were going hard at it. I don't say a word, just quietly close the door over and walk back downstairs.

Once downstairs, I tell her mother what I have seen, and that I'm leaving to go home.

I never spoke to Lisa for years after that, and her mother stopped coming to visit, I think she was embarrassed by her daughter's actions.

Now my mother's friend Susan and her daughter Lisa have stopped visiting; my mother is spending more time with her friend Senga. Senga is very supportive, almost like a counsellor, helping my mother through the hard times, with my mother's mental health going up and down, Senga is a shoulder on which to cry.

After talking with my father, he appears to be on his best behaviour, even treating my mother with the respect she deserves.

I still have everything bottled up inside me, and with everything happening with Lisa, I have no idea where I am going in life. I'm so confused about everything, and I start thinking maybe I should be gay, and once again I turn to drink.

I'm drinking all the time as it helps me to forget about my problems and dulls the emotions in my mind, so I drink until I pass out.

At times, when I am out with my friends, I get so drunk and become aggressive. I don't take any crap from anyone, and If anyone looks at me the wrong way, I have something to say. I'm getting into physical fights with people, for no good reason, I just don't care anymore, and I'm lashing out at everyone.

My attraction toward guys continues to get stronger, and my friends start watching porn, so I decided to watch it too. However, I find myself to be looking at the guys, and not the girls in the movies. As my friends start talking about the girls in the film, all I am thinking about is the guys. I found it so frustrating, and I felt so guilty for looking at the guys, I was disgusted with myself, I just kept blaming my feelings towards men on what my father did to me. I refused to accept the possibility that I could be gay.

Then one night I get so drunk with my friend Jenna, and she starts to tease me about being a virgin and asks if I'm gay. One thing leads to another, and I find myself trying to prove to myself and the world that I'm a straight guy. As the night goes on, and the drunker we get, the more she teases me, and just to prove a point, I end up in bed with her.

I hate the whole experience; I start to give Jenna oral sex and use my fingers to pleasure her, and there is a horrible smell coming from her. I then try to have intercourse with her; however, I just can't do it, the awful smell coming from between her legs, is disgusting; it is turning my stomach. Even if I want to do more, because of the pungent stench, I don't think I could.

Jenna is my first proper experience with a girl, and I assumed it is normal for a girl to smell like that if she is sexually stimulated.

The next day I had this horrible taste in my mouth; I could not shift it, and the smell was stuck up my nostrils. I spoke with a friend, and they informed me, it's not healthy for a girl to smell that way, and something must be wrong with Jenna.

I decided to talk to Jenna about the strange stench coming from between her legs, and I felt most uncomfortable, especially now the alcohol had worn off.

I go to her house, and we sit down on her sofa, I tell her I can't wait long as I am only passing, I ask her, can we talk about the other night? She answers, Callum, don't worry about it, we were both drunk, and these things happen, it's ok. So, I say; actually, it's not ok, I'm a bit concerned, and I don't know how to say this. You have a strange smell down there, and I can't shift it from my mouth or my nose, I'm sorry and embarrassed to ask; however, I need to know is everything ok down there.

I am shocked by her response; she starts to laugh and said, Callum, don't worry, I've already been to the doctor. Its only thrush, he has given me some tablets to take, it should clear up in a few days, really don't worry about it.

I could not believe what she had just said to me, I waited for about five more minutes then told her I had to leave. The thought of what I had done with her turned my stomach; I could not believe what I had just heard.

After the experience with Jenna, I was not interested in girls, and any time I thought of being with a girl, I felt sick thinking about the smell coming from Jenna.

My friends and I start to take this drug called sulf, and when I take the sulf, it makes me feel fantastic. It does not matter that my life is in tatters if I have sulf, I'm on top of the world.

I start to take sulf almost every day, and my friends and I all split on the cash so we can buy a large amount, my friends then sell some off and cut the rest. When I am taking the sulf, nothing else matters, it is excellent, and we all think we are invincible.

Then I start to run out of money and still owe money for the sulf I had got on the tick.

The problem with sulf is, when you stop taking it, your emotions spiral downward, and you go into a deep depression, it can last for days, or until you got your next fix.

I can no longer afford to buy the drugs, and I go into this terrible depression. All those horrible thoughts, the drugs and the alcohol had suppressed, suddenly they all came flooding back. Everything is at the forefront of my mind, and there is nothing I can do to change it.

Once again, I find myself back standing on that bridge, I just stand there staring at the river below, and the stars in the sky. I want it to end, and I have made my mind up, I am going to kill myself. I stand there for hours watching the water and thinking of all the reasons why I am better off dead.

The sexual abuse, the beatings, my mother's illness, the bulling, my grandparent's deaths, not being able to talk with my gran because of Peg Leg, Lisa and the baby, my confusion about my sexuality, my sister has left, and my quitting at school.

I think my father was right, I will never amount to anything, I have nothing to live for, my life is a disaster, and all I do is drink and take drugs. I then started to think of my grandparents, as I look at the stars. It is almost like I can feel them right here with me.

After a long time of standing on that bridge, and having multiple conversations with myself, thinking I am talking with my grandparents. I decided to walk away from the bridge, and I swore to myself and made a promised to my grandparents, I will sort my life out, and never touch another drug. I made a choice that day; it was to live and to make something of my life, I will prove my father wrong.

The Bridge

After the night on the bridge, something changed in me, during the week I make myself a bunch of CVs. I walk around every shop, hotel, and factory in the area; thinking someone has got to hire me. A few weeks passed, and I don't hear anything back, so I start phoning around the companies. I ask if they will take me on, and I offered to work voluntarily to start, and if they were happy with my progress, they could employ me.

It's not long before I got a phone call from a five-star hotel looking to hire me in the housekeeping department. Its only weekends to start, and my job will be cleaning the lodges. However, if things go well, and I am willing, there will be overtime available through the week, I jump at the opportunity and accept the job.

About two weeks pass before I start working in the five-star hotel, I am so excited this will be my first job. I can now prove that I am not just a waste of space to my father; I will make something of myself and prove him wrong.

The housekeeping department is hard work; my shift started at nine and finished at three-thirty. My work hours are ideal, meaning I can also keep working on my paper run, and bring in extra cash. My new job is tough, and every detail must be checked and rechecked, If the slightest thing is out of place or has the smallest mark, I need to go back and re-clean it. If it were the bedding, even a pimple sized dot on it; I get told to strip and remake the bed. Everything is on a timer and has to be ready for the next guest checking in. There is no time even to stop and think; it's just go go go, all the time. The job is very monotonous and draining; however, I stick it out; I am determined to make something of myself and prove my father wrong.

I thrive while working in the hotel, it is fantastic, I love getting out of the house, and away from my father, to earn money. I get up at five every morning to do my papers, then walk the three miles to start in the hotel at nine. I always offer to wait on late and help or to clean up the storage sheds and assist with any extra jobs; I tend to work late most nights helping.

Before long, my boss makes me an offer, she asks, will I give up my paper run, and take over the milk run on the hotel's estate. The job will be separate from my current position, and I will be paid an additional wage on top of my regular salary. Also, will I be interested in a full-time post, working five days over seven with a contract and holiday pay? I accepted without any hesitation and gave my notice to the shop keeper where I did my paper's.

I can't believe my luck, my confidence shoots through the roof, and I have some self-worth for the first time in my life.

My boss is a powerful and confident woman she has so much strength and determination within her. She never shows any sign of weakness, and I look up to her. I start thinking to myself; I want to be like that one day full of pride and self-confidence.

Once I start my new fulltime position, stop my papers and start delivering the milk, life is much more relaxed and comfortable. In my new role, I get to self-check my work; however, if something goes wrong, I have to explain to my boss why. Swapping my three big heavy paper bags and walking in the rain, sleet and snow for three hours to the one-hour milk run with an enclosed golf cart, for double the cash is a game-changer.

One of the women I work with is named Shelby, and I never give Shelby much attention at work; she is twenty years older than me and has a separate group of friends. Shelby always sits with her friends at lunch, and I sit with mine.

One day I come home from work and Shelby is sitting in my kitchen, she is drinking a bottle of wine with my mother. I instantly recognised her, so I say, oh my god I work with you, what are you doing in my house? Shelby starts to laugh and replies, it's you he is talking about, you are his brother, you are the guy I work with, now it all makes sense. I stand there just staring at her, I have a complete puzzled look on my face, waiting for an explanation!

As it turns out, my deaf brother Steve, and Shelby's daughter Jodie have been dating for several months. My brother Steve wanted to introduce Jodie's mother to my mother, so he invited her round to our house. My brother Steve had tried to explain to Shelby that his brother worked with her in the same hotel. However, with my brother being deaf, she struggled to translate the sign language and never correctly understood him. Once Shelby seen me in the kitchen, everything became apparent, and she knew what my brother had been trying to sign to her.

Shelby started to visit our house regularly, and she and my mother would talk and have a few drinks in the kitchen. At the same time, my father played his computer in the living room. The more I spoke with Shelby at my mothers, the more I got to know her, and we started to talk in work and become friends.

A friend of mine lets me down with a holiday, at the last minute she cancelled out on me. The holiday got paid in full, so rather than losing the money, or cancelling the holiday altogether, Shelby offers to come on holiday with me.

I am now nineteen, and Shelby is thirty-nine, this will be my second holiday ever, I have never been abroad, or on a plane, I am so nervous. The last holiday I had was with my sister, at the holiday camp for families with problems, the place where I got bullied, and my sister got punched on her face.

We go to Tenerife, and my worrying is all for nothing, it is a fabulous holiday. I have so much fun, we both get so drunk, I am starting to feel alive for the first time in my life. Then we met these two gay guys; they are both single and very handsome, and we all decide to go on a night out together, we go to a few clubs and pubs along the beach, and we are all having so much fun. As the night goes on, Shelby got tired and decided to go to bed, leaving me alone with them, and I ended up going back to their apartment for more drinks.

When I am alone with them, I asked them loads of questions about being gay, it's a fantastic night, and I instantly click with the two guys; they make me feel so comfortable. I get so drunk and open up to them, and then I passed out on their sofa. Nothing happened, I just fell asleep, when I wake in the morning, I'm thinking, where the hell am I? then it all comes back to me, I don't wake the guys, I just quietly leave.

When I return to our apartment, I find Shelby sitting waiting for me, she starts to chuckle then says, so Callum, have you got something to tell me? I ask, like what? What do you mean! Shelby then says to me, she knew I was gay all along, and it is ok she won't tell anyone; what happens on holiday, stays on holiday. I get myself into such a panic, and I try explaining to her, I am not gay, I passed out on their sofa, and nothing happened, I only spoke to the guys, fuck sake is it a crime to talk to a gay guy. I ignore her for the rest of the day, and I tell her that I'm angry at her for accusing me of being gay.

The next day she tells me she is sorry and that she was only joking with me. She then says I never meant to upset you, and I promised not to wind you up anymore, so can we be friends and enjoy the rest of our holiday together. I accept her apology, and we have a fantastic last few days' in Tenerife.

After the holiday Shelby and I become very close friends, we do everything together; It is just what I need. I start going over to Shelby's house after work, and we listen to all the old tunes over a few bottles of wine and dance around like idiots. It is good fun being friends with Shelby, and I enjoy her company. However, she never lets up about me being gay, and she keeps joking about me having two gay guys on holiday. I get so angry with her and lose my temper, and I smash a glass of wine by throwing it across her living room, I am so livid with her, and ask that she stop calling me gay, then I storm out her house in a rage.

I feel frustrated and confused in my head, without my friends adding to it. The more people that accused me of being gay, the more I feel anger towards them and my father, simply because I blame him for making me feel that way. I also feel guilty within myself for feeling gay, and I start to blow up at anyone who calls me gay. I even beat up some of the people, and I guess it was just Shelbys' turn to get shouted at from me.

A few days later, Shelby apologised to me in work, and I to her, then she asked me if I have seen the new guy that's just started. As I say nope, this overly flamboyant gay guy struts through the linin room winks at me then says, alrighty babes.

His name is Drake, Drake is very handsome and openly gay, and I am attracted to him big time; It's like a high school crush, and I want to know everything about him. I have never seen an openly gay guy before, even the two guys from holiday were very discreet; I am fascinated by him and his antics.

There is no fooling Drake, one day in the office he says to me, so babes, when are you going to come out of the closet? I just chuckle and blush, and my face got scarlet, as I answer, don't be silly; you know I'm not gay; I'm not like that.

Drake knew I was attracted to him; always telling me, if I ever decide to come out, maybe we can go on a date, then winking at me. As time goes on, I find myself regularly flirting with him.

Then one day, Drake and I are alone in the linen room, and I have my back to him filling the dryers. When he sneaked up behind me and leaned in so close; I could feel his lips on my ear, as he whispers, nice butt handsome as he slid his hand down, touching my bottom. Instantly I flashback to my father abusing me and I completely lose it, I spin around and push him away from me, then I punch him. As he falls back and lands on the concrete floor, I towered over him shouting; don't you ever fucking touch me again; do you hear me, just get it into your thick head I'm no poof. I then storm out of the linen room and avoid Drake for the rest of the day.

The next day Drake is sitting in the linen room, I feel terrible for what I did and how I have reacted; after all, I was flirting with him.

I approach Drake and apologise, telling him I'm sorry for my behaviour, I was out of line yesterday and overreacted. I have some personal issues, and I am trying to deal with them. Drake makes a joke of the situation, then does that special little wink. Drake then says, he will accept my apology, but only if I make a deal with him, he asks that I go with him to a gay club. Then says, Babe if you come to the club, you can find out who you are, and if I'm wrong, I will drop it, I promise I won't bring it up again, then he blew me a kiss and did his cheeky little wink again.

Drake is very laid back about being gay; he takes everything in his stride and is very persuasive. So, I decided I will visit the gay club with Drake and our work colleagues; I think perhaps Drake is right, and I might just find my true self.

As we arrived at the club, the big bodybuilder on the door slaps Drake's bottom and says, Drake, I will see you later and makes a rude gesture with his mouth, tongue and hand. As we walk inside the club, my eyes are everywhere; It is like a different world. There are guys kissing guys, guys dancing with guys, guys holding hands, even guys dressed in full drag. Everyone just accepts each other, and I'm mesmerised with my surroundings. As the night goes on, we all get drunk, and I become more relaxed, with everyone in the club knowing Drake, they all make sure I feel welcome. When I go to the toilet, Drake tells James, his friend, to make sure I am ok.

James stops me on the steps as I exit the bathroom and we got talking. Because I have drunk quite a bit, I get upset and open up to James, and I explain how I'm confused with my sexuality. I find it comfortable talking with James with him being a stranger. James comforts me and tells me how he has gone through the same emotions, then he looks at me and asks me to kiss him, so we briefly kiss, and he asks, did that feel right? I answer him and say yes it did, it felt right, and I feel comfortable with you. Then James said well there's your answer as he cuddles me and says we better get back to the table and joined the others.

As the night continued, Drake went to the toilet several times to carry out sexual acts, each time with different guys. As I observe my surroundings, the more I see things happening, the more everything seems sleazy. As the night goes on, even James has gone to the bathroom for some dirty fun a few times. I start to dislike being in the gay club and think very little of Drake and his friends with the things they are doing. As the evening ended, I became uncomfortable and glad to get out of there and go home.

The next day in work, Drake approaches me and asks, so babes, have you figured out just who you are? I reply I'm not sure that's the life for me, I kind of felt uncomfortable, if I'm honest. Drake started to laugh and says; it's a real shame the photographs don't say that. I look directly at Drake, and I ask, what are you talking about, what pictures? Drake tells me, one of our work colleagues has taken some snapshots of our night out, and there are pictures of me kissing his friend James. He says, Callum, in the pictures it looks to me like you were having a great night, and he starts laughing. I go into a blind panic, and I ask, who has the photographs and who has seen them? I need those photos back, and I need you guys not to say anything to anyone, this is not funny, this is my life.

I am not ready for the world to know I am gay, so I beg my colleagues to give me the pictures and not to say anything.

My work colleagues don't tell anyone; however, it has been a few days, and they continue refusing to provide me with the photos. I end up breaking down and telling my friends Dianne and Sarah what has happened, and how I'm so embarrassed about everything and feel so stupid. I am still terrified of my father, and the last thing I want is him finding out I kissed another guy, so my two friends decide to help me.

Dianne and Sarah go to the colleague's house, and with a bit of forced persuasion, manage to convince the work colleague to destroy the pictures and keep it quiet. I feel like a black cloud has lifted from over me; however, people were still whispering and gossiping among themselves.

I decide to tell Shelby about visiting the gay club, and all the things that happened, with James and the pictures. Shelby is so angry about the pictures and excited about my experience. She said, I knew you were gay, I've always known; even before you went with those two gay guys on holiday. I started to laugh at her, and once again, I explained, how many times do I need to tell you, I never went with the gay guys on holiday, I was just confused back then.

A few months have passed since visiting the gay club, and I have told a small circle of close friends, I think I might be gay. My circle of friends ask that I return to the club; this time with them, they believe my experience will be different if I'm there with genuine friends. I am against the idea at first; then I decided to go back to the gay club with them.

I'm nervous about going back to the club, and self-conscious with my skin as it has got worse with psoriasis. This time I feel things will be different as I'm going to the club knowing I want to be gay, I'm not confused, and I want to do this, I needed to get it out of my system.

As we arrive in the gay club, I feel comfortable, and I'm confident having my friends with me. As the night goes on, a guy buys me a couple of drinks, and is chatting with me; his name is Andrew.

Andrew is thirty-one, and I am nineteen, it is evident that Andrew works out; his body is perfect, and he is very handsome. We chat over some drinks, then we both danced; he is a gentleman, and never once asked for dirty fun in the toilet.

As the evening comes to an end, Andrew invites myself and all my friends back to his place for some drinks, my friends approve of him, and we all accepted the invitation.

In the taxi, arriving at his flat, my friends warn him, he better be gentle with me, and no funny business. Andrew just gives me a cheeky smile as he looks at me and says, well that's entirely up to Callum.

When we enter his flat, it is immaculate and very stylish, it has a beautiful view of the city. Sitting on his big luxury sofa, I am feeling so nervous. All I can think about is my bad skin, I still live with my parents, I'm a glorified cleaner, and I am out of my depth with him. Andrew has the perfect body, a luxury flat, a good job, and it is clear he has money.

After a few drinks and getting to know each other better, Andrew asks if I want to sleep in his bed with him or pile on to his couch with my friends? I don't even get the chance to answer, and my friend Dianne shouts, well, if Callum does not come into that bed with you, I am coming into it with you. At the same time, she is nudging me toward his bedroom door.

In his bedroom, Andrew is so gentle with me, he makes everything feel right, and I'm comfortable with him. For the first time in my life, I never thought about my father touching me, and being gay never felt dirty or wrong. Andrew knows I'm new to the gay scene, and he tells me he will not have sex with me, not on our first date, my first time should be a pleasant experience, and that I should not just have sex with the first guy I meet on a night out. We both explored every other thing you can imagine doing other than penetrative sex; Andrew is very experienced and knows how to please.

The next morning when I wake, all my friends have gone; they must have got a taxi during the night. Andrew makes a lovely breakfast for both of us, and over breakfast, he tells me he enjoyed my company, then gives me his phone number and asked that I keep in touch.

The night with Andrew is one of the best nights of my life, and it changes how I view being gay and makes things clear for me, I no longer feel ashamed or disgusting for my attraction to guys.

When I get home, I feel overcome with happiness, and I can't wait to tell my circle of friends about what happened with Andrew.

After I talk to my friends and explain how I feel, my friends encouraged me to call him. However, as much as I want to call, I am just too nervous, and keep putting it off.

About two-month pass since the night out with Andrew and I'm at a party with my friends. At the party, all I can talk about is my night with Andrew and how amazing it was. The more I get drunk, the more I tell my friends, I want to phone him, but I'm still too nervous. Throughout the night, my friends keep pushing me to call him; eventually, I work up the courage and make the call. I am so nervous when Andrew answers, and I stutter down the phone, Hi Andrew, this is Callum, I am not sure if you remember me? Andrew replies, of course, I can remember you, I spent the night with you! Is everything ok, why did you not call me? I avoid the answer by saying; I'm out at a party, do you want to meet up with me? Andrew replied I'm sorry Callum, I told you I'm not a one-night kind of guy, it has been over two months, and you did not call; I thought you were not interested and now I have met someone. I'm so embarrassed by the whole thing and feel like a complete idiot, I say sorry for disturbing him, and then I hang up the phone.

After the party and everything that happened with Andrew, I decide I don't want to live in my mother's house anymore. I find it too challenging living in the same house as my father, acting or even thinking about being gay around my father, just feels dirty. I don't want to give my father an excuse to try anything with me or touch me again, and just looking at him makes me feel sick. My emotions are all over the place, and although I have not fully come out as being gay, I needed to get out of there; It is time to get my own home.

I apply to the council for my own house; however, not living in cramped accommodation, having children or any disability, the council place me at the bottom of the housing. It could be months or even years before I can get my place. I decide my best option is to buy a house and set up a meeting with the local estate agents and bank. Unfortunately, the bank tells me my wages are too low, and I don't qualify for a mortgage; I'm devastated, and I feel so trapped.

I apply to several jobs in the area, and eventually, get offered a full-time job as a supervisor in a retail shop. I jump at the chance as its better pay and will help me to get more cash for a mortgage.

I work in the shop for just over a month, and everything is going great. Then both the assistant manager and the manager decide to hand in their notice. In their absence, the regional manager comes to run the store, while she is running the store, she promotes me to assistant manager. I am so happy with my promotion and eager to prove my worth; this could be my opportunity to become a store manager. The regional manager worked alongside me for a month; she assisted me with the running of the store, teaching me everything then offered me the manager's position, I accepted. I feel proud of myself, and I'm now earning enough money to buy my place.

My father is always saying; I will never amount to anything in life. With my new manager's position, I feel like I have proved him wrong, and I am a success.

I make another appointment with the bank and talk with the mortgage broker, and receive excellent news, I got accepted. I can finally escape from my father and get my own house, and be openly gay If I want to be.

I purchase a one-bedroom flat opposite my work, and I move in within a few months. Moving into the new flat I have nothing, life is tough, and I sleep on the floor for the first few weeks, and then I get everything on hire purchase, money is very tight. However, I have a good job that I enjoyed, and with my new home, I am finally free from my father.

After a few months in my new flat, I start to think about my brothers and feel so guilty for leaving them, what if my father starts to touch them as he did to me. I can't ever return to that house and will never tell anyone that my father is a beast, and I know It is selfish of me to leave, and not talk out, but I am just so scared of the consequences. I don't want to hurt my mother or tear our family apart, and that's if she even believed me anyway. I'm so confused and don't know what to do, so I selfishly block everything out and just get on with my life.

I know that I'm leaving my mother and brothers at risk, and I feel so guilty. Trying to forget everything and block it all out, I find myself going to parties and once again drinking until I pass out. That's when I met Clay, Clay is sixteen, and I'm nineteen, we are both closet gays, and only our closest friends know we are gay. Clay and I seem to get on well; he is nothing like Andrew; however, we do share the fact we were both discreet gay guys.

Clay works as a waiter and goes to college, he is very sexually active and has sexual relations with many different guys, despite him being so young. I'm apprehensive at first and do not want to start a relationship. However, he is very persistent and shows lots of interest in me; It feels good having someone attracted to me and paying me some attention. Clay accepted my skin condition, which makes me feel comfortable with him, so I agree to start dating him.

After a few months of dating, we decided to come out and tell the world we are gay, including our parents. His family go crazy; they blame me for their son being gay, and just hate me from the get-go. Clay still lives with his parents, and I have my flat. It's a challenging relationship for us both, our families don't get along, and his parents don't make it easy for me. Still, we stick it out and get through it together.

It has been two years since I moved out of my parents, and I try my best not to talk to my father. However, I still talk to my mother, and she comes to visit me from time to time.

One night, I'm sitting alone in my flat, my front door gets chapped, and thinking its Clay I just swing the door open, it's my father standing at the door drunk as ever and asking to come in. I instantly begin to shake and become nervous, as I hesitantly tell him, I am just about to go out. My father says, I've had a little argument with your mother and have nowhere to go, please let me stay with you; I promise you won't even know I'm here.

My heart sunk, and I can feel the colour drain from my face. I start thinking about my poor mother, hoping he has not beaten her. Somehow, I pluck up the courage and say Dad, can you please go away, you are not welcome here, and you know the reason why. I see his facial expression change instantly, from smug smirk to angry frown. He says, now Callum, that's not very nice treating your dad like that, I've already told you I'm sorry for what I did, I can't turn back time. I just say to him, I'm sorry and quickly close the front door over and lock it. I can hear him pacing back and forth outside the door, I close all my blinds and curtains and sit there in my flat terrified and shaking.

After about an hour, I no longer hear him pacing, so I sneak to the door and peep through the spy hole, I'm afraid, and my heart is racing. He must have spotted me, he lifts the letterbox, and begins shouting, I'm still here are you going to let me in, I'm not going to do anything, I just need somewhere to sleep.

Thankfully, I can hear the neighbour across the landing come out, and he asks my father why he has been hanging around for over an hour. My father says to him, I've just come to visit my son, but I guess I'm not welcome here. The neighbour then says to him, yes that seems about right, I don't think you are, so I think you should leave now, don't you? After the neighbour speaks with him, I can hear my father going; he slams the close door then shouts something as he punched the bins sitting outside my window.

It has been four years since my father last sexually assaulted me, and in that instant, everything came flooding back. I'm devastated, and I think I am never going to be free from him, I just sit in my living room crying and feeling like that scared little boy from my childhood all over again. I hate my father, and I hate living there on my own, knowing that he can turn up at any time.

Clay and I have been together as a couple for two years, and later that night when Clay comes to visit, I'm so upset. I explain to Clay everything that happened with my father growing up, including being sexually abused. I told Clay I did not feel safe living alone and asked him to move in with me. That night I begged Clay never to do or say anything about what I have told him, and that I never want to discuss it again. Clay agrees, then tells his parents he is moving into my flat with me. His parents are not happy when they find out; however, Clay says to them they have no choice, it is his decision, and he is doing it whether they accept it or not.

Karen finds out I have my own house and she decides to visit. When she arrived, I introduced her to Clay, and Karen introduced us to her new partner Angus. I'm surprised with them as a couple, Angus is thirty years older than her; however, Karen is happy, and Angus appeared to be kind to her. During Karen's visit, she tells me her father has passed away, and both she and her mother are now talking.

Both Karen and Angus get on well with Clay, and they start to visit him regularly when I'm out at work.

Over time my relationship with Clay starts to break down, and Clay just wants more and more from me, so I start getting myself into debt to please him. I know he has started messing about with other guys behind my back, and I just turn a blind eye; because I never want to be alone in that flat again.

To keep Clay happy, I get several loans and buy him new clothes, and then I apply to get a thousand-pound overdraft from my bank. I use the overdraft to take him on holiday; I'm hoping the holiday will help our relationship get back on track.

After the holiday Clay wants a new car, and I know we can't afford it; however, I decide to get one on hire purchase for him. I am desperately trying to win his affection because I'm too scared of being alone in the flat, knowing my father could turn up any time.

Clay then loses his job, and I am trying to support both of us and run a house.

My work asks me if I can go away to assist with opening another shop; it would only take a few weeks at the most, and I will get extra cash for my troubles. Clay and I discuss it, and we decided I should go as the extra money will help us. While I'm away, I phoned Clay every night to talk to him, both Karen and Angus are there every night keeping Clay company.

When I return home from working away, my friend Shelby tells me she had come down to the house a few times and thought something was going on between Karen and Clay. She says things just did not seem right, and they were all acting strange with her.

Then one night we are out having a drink when Clay and I get into an argument, so I leave the club and come home early. When Clay arrives home a few hours later, we start to argue, and I tell Clay he has to start pulling his weight and get a job; I simply can't afford to keep both of us. As things get more heated, I ask him, do you remember that night when Shelby came down, and

I was working away, did something happen between you and Karen? He comes right out with it, and says, yes it did, we had a threesome. Karen, Angus and I had sex it's no big deal, and while I am at it, I have slept with your brother Steve, and do you remember the guy Stuart at my work? Well, I have slept with him too, and his brother.

I go into a red rage, just like I had done all those years ago with Jake. I grab Clay, and I keep hitting him over and over until he falls onto the floor, then I take the music system and smash it over his head. With Clay laid out on the floor, I march into our bedroom and start to strip the bed, I'm furious and screaming at him, why would you do this to me, and in our bed? Why, when I've done nothing but be loving to you, your nothing but a dirty bastard? Then I notice him trying to get up from the floor; his head has a gash on it and covered in blood. I charge at him from the bedroom, and he panics, he puts one foot on to my sofa and jumps right through the living room window to get away from me. I feel so angry I want to kill him.

Then the realisation of what has just happened hits me. I'm sitting on the living room floor all alone, I have smashed up my flat, there is glass everywhere, and I have no window. My brother and my life long best friend have both slept with my partner, and now it is officially over with Clay, and I'm going to be all alone in my flat.

The next day his parents come down to collect his belongings, and they don't say much; however, the looks I get from them said it all. Clay has officially moved back into his parent's house, and he is entirely debt-free. Me on the other hand, have been left with a pile of debt, and a new car to pay, when I don't even have a driving licence, and the one thing I feared the most, I'm now alone in my flat.

When I confronted my brother about sleeping with Clay, he admits it. He says, he is sorry, and that it happened when they were both drunk, and I had Passed out, it was just a stupid mistake, and he wishes it never happened. It is my disabled brother, and I want to punch fuck out of him so much. However, because of all his operations, he can't take hits to his head, so I hold myself back. My mother defends him as I confront him and asks me to drop it. If not for my mother and his disability, I would have beaten him; I'm so angry with him; it takes everything I have to restrain myself.

I'm also so angry with Karen for what she has done to me, and I just keep thinking. She has been my closest friend since childhood, why would she do this to me, we have always been there for each other, and I just can't understand it.

A few days later and there is a chap at the door, I get such a fright and instantly think it could be my father, so from behind the locked door, I shout who is it, I'm relieved to hear Karen's mothers voice. She asks if she can come in and talk with me about everything that's happened.

Once I let Glenda in, she says, Karen is embarrassed with what she has done to you. She is heartbroken, and she doesn't want to see your friendship end. Karen has said she is sorry for everything and asks will you please talk to her. I tell Glenda I need some time to get my head around all this, and when I am ready, I will come to see Karen.

A few months pass, and I phone Glenda, and I ask that she tell Karen to come and visit me, I'm ready to chat with her if she still wants to talk.

Not even an hour goes passed, and there is a chap at the door; Its Karen wanting to talk about things. We sit for about two hours talking about growing up together, and how we should not let her stupid mistake destroy a two-decade friendship. I tell Karen I need some time to heal. However, I do forgive her for what she did to me, and we can now be friends.

Karen and I become closer than ever; it's like she is trying to make up for the wrong she did to me; I guess she felt guilty.

Karen and Angus move home, and the new house is on the same street as my friend Shelby, considering everything that has happened, we are all getting on fantastic.

One-night Karen is sitting with me in my living room, and my phone starts to ring. I answer, and at first, there is no one on the other end, then the phone rings again, I answer, this time someone is heavy breathing on the other end, then it is just this high pitch laugh. I think nothing of it and hang up the phone.

A few days later and the car that I can't drive starts getting scratches on it. I tell Karen and Shelby that something is not right, I keep getting crank Phone calls, and now someone is scratching my car; It's starting to concern me. Both Shelby and Karen come down to comfort me, they reassure me everything is going to be ok, and it's probably just some kids playing pranks on me. Having no known enemy, I have got it into my head; it can only be two people, my father or Clay.

The phone calls continue, then one day it happens when Karen is in the flat with me. Karen answered the phone, and she tells me that they say to her, tell Callum I am going to get him, and I know when he is home alone. Karen slams the phone down, then says, it sounded like your father, it was an older guy, there is no way it can be Clay.

I start to get super paranoid, and with every noise I hear, I'm up at my window, and I'm getting very little sleep.

Then a few days later, I wake up to find someone has posted gay magazines to all my neighbour's windows and plastered them on to all the car windscreens. All have attached to them a compliment's sticker from, Callum at number 35.

I am so embarrassed and have to go into the street and peel all the gay pictures from my neighbour's windows and cars. I can see everyone is looking at me from there windows, I get distraught about the whole thing, and I can't sleep at night, I know it is my father.

When I tell Karen what has happened, she is livid and tells me she will be right down. When she arrives at the flat, Karen gives me a huge cuddle, and she reassures me everything is going to be all right and that she is here for me. She says when she finds out who has done this, she will take care of the culprit once and for all.

I have not slept for days and decided to purchase a security camera in the hope of catching the culprit. I position the hidden camera discreetly pointing it toward my car, and I'm convinced I will see my father or Clay on the camera. I try to stay awake that night and watch the security screen; however, due to lack of sleep over the past few weeks, I can't, and I fall asleep at three in the morning and wake at eight.

The next day, my car has scratches all over it again, so I check the camera back from three o'clock. I get a hit on the camera at three-thirty, at first, I see the headlight of a car, they stop just out of range of my camera and window. A few seconds later, I see Karen and Angus appear; I think they must be doing their rounds to make sure I'm ok. Then it becomes clear, they are not there for me at all, Karen starts sticking gay posters to the car, and Angus is rubbing it with sandpaper. Karen then starts sticking the Posters to all the vehicles next to mine. I can't believe my eyes, and I feel sick.

All this time Karen convinced me it was my father, she knew I was terrified he was going to come and get me, so much for our two-decade friendship. Then I thought back to the phone calls, and how she was sitting there with me when I received them, she knew it was her partner Angus on the other end of the phone, yet led me to believe it was my father.

I am furious, and I go straight to her house, I throw the posters at her and say, I got you on C.C.T.V. Karen, you and Angus. Our friendship is over, and if you ever bother me again, I'm giving the footage to the police.

I am so angry at myself, and I should never have spoken to her after everything she did to me with Clay; I feel so stupid for for-giving her. Karen moved away after what she did, and our friend-ship ended for good, and I never had any more crank calls or magazines posted in the street.

I'm in debt up to my eyes; I've been eating soup and porridge for months, and I'm jumping every time someone chaps my door.

When I think things can't get any worse, my regional manager turns up at my store, and she has a pile of letters in her hand; they're for all the staff. As she hands me the letters, she apolo-gises. Then says, I've come to the store today, to answer any queries you might have, regarding the information enclosed within the letter.

The letter stated our store is not making enough money to cover the rent and wage costs; therefore, they will be closing the store down and shipping out all our stock. My boss then says, Callum, your store will close in three months, and you will receive a redundancy package, one week's pay for each year you have worked for the company. It will include holiday pay for the remainder of this year. I truly am sorry, it's for the needs of the business and was not my decision.

The three months pass, and I'm made redundant, I can't afford to keep my house, so I place it on to the market. The council said they will not rehouse me, as I still own my flat. I can't pay my mortgage as I have no job, and with no money, I can't buy food gas or electricity. I have no way out, the thought of having to go back to my mothers, knowing my father is there, terrified me. I have hit rock bottom, and I feel like a complete failure.

Within this year, I have lost my boyfriend, my best friend, my brother, my job and soon my house. Not knowing what to do or where to turn, as usual, I hit the drink big time, I'm drinking every day and every night. Everything has become too much to bear, and I finally broke down as I just can't take it anymore, so I decided to go to Shelby's house, as I need a friend. I'm sobbing my heart out to her, telling her I have lost everything, and I don't want to go back to my mother's house. Then it all starts to come out, one thing after another, I'm telling her, he will do it again, he will touch me, I can't go back there. Shelby, I hate him, he has sexually abused me for years, please Shelby help me, I don't know what to do.

I finally speak out about all those years of sexual abuse at the hands of my father. Shelby gives me the biggest cuddle and says, Callum, tell me what has happened, you know you can talk to me about anything.

I'm sobbing my heart out like I did that day in primary school with Mrs Fraser, and I'm trying to tell Shelby, but I'm so upset and what I'm trying to say is all coming out in bits and pieces. I'm saying to her, he wanted to push me from the cliff, he touches me, hits me when I sleep; he has a key for the door; I can't stop him, I can't go back, please Shelby, I just can't.

Once calm, I clearly explain everything to Shelby, and She says to me, Callum; you have to tell your mother, she has to know about your father, for your little brother's sake. As soon as she mentioned my brothers, I have this instant feeling of guilt come over me; I think back to when I moved out and had first left them. I sit with Shelby for several hours, pleading with her to keep it a secret, but she just keeps saying, Callum, I cannot do that; it's not only you at risk; you have to think of your little brothers. You have to tell her, and she hands me the phone, saying call your mother, ask her to come to my house, as you need to talk with her.

I start pressing the phone buttons so slowly, and I'm shaking with nerves and crying so hard. I'm thinking about all the things my father has told me will happen if I ever say anything. I don't want my mother going back into the psychiatric ward, or my brothers getting put in to care. Still, at the same time, I have Shelby right in front of me, encouraging me to make the call, and telling me it's the right thing to do.

When my mother answers the telephone, I'm crying, and say, mum, I need to tell you something, can you please come over to Shelby's house. Please don't bring my father with you, and don't tell him you are coming here, you must be alone it's important; I then hang the phone up.

I am so afraid, and my whole body is shaking, I know for the first time in years, I'm about to get his dirty secret off my chest. My emotions are all over the place, and I start to think about how I will tell my mum, I have a million thoughts running through my head. I'm panicking and scared, thinking I will say the wrong thing, and she won't believe me. I start pleading with Shelby again, and saying, please I can't do this, what if she doesn't believe me, or if she takes a breakdown and it's all my fault? What if my father comes with her? Shelby, I can't do it.

Then I hear the close buzzer, and It feels like someone has frozen time; this silence and stillness came over me, and the buzz sounds like the loudest noise in the world, I know it is my mother at the door; she has arrived. My heart sinks, I know what I'm about to do and say will change the lives of everyone close to me forever.

CHAPTER NINE
Age 20 to 40

TELLING MOTHER

When my mother arrives, I am trying so hard to tell her, but I just can't get the words out, I keep looking at her, and the tears are streaming down my face. My mother sits on the sofa next to me and asks, Callum what is wrong, what has happened? I keep stuttering at her, but I just can't bring myself to say it.

Then I say, I'm sorry mum, I love you, I then put my head in my hands and pause for a second, and my mother is asking, what has happened? Callum, it's alright just talk to me.

I start to force the words out, he has been doing things to me, and I am sorry I could not stop him, I'm sorry mum, I could not tell you, I could not tell anyone.

My mother starts to shake her head in diss belief; I think she knows what's coming next. My mother asks, who did these things, and what things did they do to you? Then I tell her.

My father, he has been touching me; it started when I was just a young child. My mother's eyes begin to fill with tears, she is shaking her head sobbing and saying no no no, what do you mean by he was touching you?

I begin to tell her; he would sneak into my room and do things to me at night. He did it when you were sleeping, or when you went out to nans or when you were getting shopping, and when you were in the hospital; I'm sorry mum he has done it a lot. Then I start sobbing and put my hands over my face; I can't look at my mother as I feel disgusting and ashamed about what has happened.

My mother begins crying and saying, no not you, not my boy,

how could he do this to you, why would he do this? I'm sorry Callum if I've not been there for you, I'm your mother, and I should have been there to protect you.

I just keep telling her; it's not her fault; it was him that did this to me, and not her.

My mother's mood then changes, and she goes into a rage, she starts shouting, that dirty bastard, how could he do that to you, I'm going to fucking kill him, I will slit the bastard's throat and do time for him. Then she starts to break down again and says; I'm sorry for not being there when you needed me, how could I let this happen to you.

She is going between rage at him, and pain for me, and feeling guilty for not being there to protect me; her emotions are all over the place.

Then she wants to leave Shelby's house to confront him; telling me, she is going to kill him, I beg her to wait in Shelby's as I am scared for her safety. My mother is no match for my father, so I lock the house door, removing the keys and placing them into my pocket, and refuse to let my mother leave. I am scared that my father will hurt her, or twist her mind to believe him over me, the same way he did with the teachers.

My mother is being hysterical, and then she looks at me and asks, why have you not said anything before now, I don't understand if this has gone on for years, why wouldn't you tell me?

I say to her, do you remember that time with the school, when my father told you I was jealous, and upset because Steve was in the hospital and getting all the attention? My mother says, yes that's right, your father had to go up to the school and talk to the headteacher because you were so upset! Then I say, my father forced me to say I was jealous and that I was lying. What I said to the teachers that day was the truth about what was happening, and my father twisted everything. Then there was that day that I hid under the washing basket in the kitchen, I was hysterical and begging for you to take me with you to nanas house, can you remember that? My mother replies, yes, of course, I remember it, but you always wanted to come with me.

I tell her, well, he did it to me that day, so is it any wonder why I wanted to be with you all the time, I knew he was going to do it, and that's why I was so adamant about wanting to come with you. My father told me when I was just young that he would throw me off the cliff if I said anything. He also said you would be angry at me, or even go back into the psychiatric hospital. I didn't want to hurt you or have our family broken up, and my brothers put into care, I was just so scared, I'm sorry for not telling you. I did try to tell the teachers in primary school, and I got into trouble for lying.

My mother puts her face in her hands and starts crying, then says twenty-eight years I have been with that bastard, I can't believe this is happening. I just don't understand why you never told me sooner, Callum, I'm your mother, you should have said something to me.

I look at her angrily and say, why did you let him hit us? And what about Peg Leg, I told you about him, and you never believed me, you just sent me back over to my gran's house, with him there, you just let it all happen, why?

My mother brakes down again and starts sobbing, she just keeps saying, I'm sorry, I was not there for you, I have let you down and should have been there for you.

I start to explain myself again and say; it's not your fault he did this, and he told me, if I said anything, It would make you ill. You would need to leave us and go back to the hospital, I never wanted to hurt you, so I kept quiet. My mother is sobbing so hard and opens her arms to hold me, she grips me tight in her arms, hugging me and repeatedly saying I am sorry I was not there for you.

Then my mother's sorrow turns to anger again, and she starts to beg me for the keys to confront my father. I refuse point blank to give her the keys and say, you can't go back to the house; I am too scared for your safety.

My mother decides to phone him, and when he answers, she shouts, how could you do that to our son, you dirty bastard, twenty-eight years we have been married, we have five children together, what is wrong with you, and why have you done this?

My father replies in a calm voice; I am sorry Mary, I never meant to hurt you, I do love you and the kids, please Tell Callum I'm sorry for hurting him. I don't know why I did it to him, I can't change what I've done, and I can only say I'm sorry to all of you and Callum.

My mother then shouts, but why I don't understand, why did you do it, what's wrong with you?

My father says, Mary, you know what my brother did to me growing up, and I know that's no excuse, but I think that's why I did it to Callum, please tell him I'm sorry.

My mother then starts roaring down the phone at him; I fucking hate you, get all of your shit together and get out of my house, I never want to see you again.

My father replies calmly, Mary, I understand, and I'm sorry for what I've done, I promise you I will be out of the house by the time you arrive home. I do love you, and I am sorry, then he hangs up the phone.

A few moments later, and Shelby's buzzer rings again, I go into such a panic; I think it's my father at the door. Shelby answered her intercom in the hall and shouted through to the lounge, Mary it's alright its only your Beth at the door, so I've let her in. Now knowing it is not my father, everyone takes a sigh of relief.

As my sister enters the lounge, my mother starts crying and breaks down to my sister, explaining everything I have just told her. My sister is furious and asks, where is he, where is that dirty bastard, I want to ask him what the fuck is going on in his head.

My mother says, Beth, he is leaving, I have asked him to pack his bags and go, I think he will be gone now.

My sister looks to myself and my mother with a confused look and asks, what the fuck do you mean gone, gone where? My mother tells her again, I have asked him to leave the house, I told him to take his stuff and get out, I've said to him it's over, and I never want to see him again.

My sister is livid with everything and decides she too will phone him, and when he answers, she asks, why did you do it, what the fuck is wrong with you, Are you gay, Are you a pervert. How the fuck could you do that to our Callum? My father says I'm sorry for what I have done to Callum, and I'm sorry for hurting you all, I have left the house now, so you won't ever need to see me again. Please tell your mother and brothers that I'm sorry for everything. Then he hangs up, and my sister tries to call him back; however, he does not answer.

We sit in Shelby's for the rest of the night and speak about things it is so emotional. My sister asks, Callum why have you never said anything? You should have come to me. I try to explain to her; there were so many reasons for not speaking out, my father had told me not to say anything, and I was so scared of him, mum was unwell, and I did not want to make her worse. I even spoke out to the school, and he twisted things, making me be in the wrong and not him, he threatened to throw me off the top of a cliff, I was just so scared that no one would believe me, Karen's father, Peg Leg and our uncle bobby, all of them walked free for the same thing, so why would this be any different?

My sister tells me to phone the police and get him charged for what he has done to me. I tell her I don't want to get the police involved, and that I just want to forget about everything, he has gone now, and it's all over.

My sister gets angry and asks, what do you mean it is all over? Then she says, Callum, this might be over for you, and off your chest, but this is just us finding out about all of this happening to you. There is no way you can let him get away with this, and there is no way I'm allowing him to get away with it.

I start crying and say to my sister; you don't understand what will happen if I talk to the police. I will need to give a statement, and that will mean going over every dirty detail about what he did to me. I can't face that torture in my mind, I have spent my entire life trying to block this shit out, and now you want me to go through it all again, well I'm not doing it.

After a few hours and talking through everything with my mother, my sister and my good friend Shelby, I decide to contact the police. The three of them convince me this is something I have to do, not only for me but to protect others from my father. If my father walks free, he can hurt more children, and we all need justice for what he did to our family; we need to make sure he can't hurt anyone else in the future.

My father wastes no time, and when my mother arrives home, he has packed all his things leaving nothing. He has taken all the money from the house and left my mother with nothing.

A few days later, my mother goes to the bank, only to discover he has emptied the bank account and closed it. My father has taken every penny and left my mother with absolutely nothing; she can't even afford to feed herself or my brothers.

It takes the police about a week to trace my father and arrest him. After the police have interviewed my father, they informed me how the interview went. The police tell me that my father was very cocky and sure of himself. He said to them the whole thing was a misunderstanding and it's a load of nonsense and make belief by his son Callum.

The police take further statements from everyone involved and question my father a few more times. When the police have investigated the matter, and confident they have enough evidence gathered to build the case against him; they hand everything over to the procurator's fiscal office.

It takes the fiscal's office about a month to look over my case, and once they have come to a decision, the police come to my work to inform me of the next step, I'm shocked with what the police say. The procurator fiscal's office has concluded, that due to the lack of sufficient evidence, the case will not go to court. The officers then tell me, we find this happens a lot with these historical cases of sexual abuse.

I am confused and upset, and I ask the police, how can this be possible, my father admitted it. You have the statements to prove it from my mother and sister, he confessed to both of them on the telephone.

The police reply, I am sorry Callum, your father's defence lawyer looked over the statements. He stated that at no point in time did anyone use the words sexual abuse during the phone calls to your father. His lawyer has pointed out it is clear they all ask how your father could do what he did to you. Your sister asks him what his sexual orientation is, but none of them actually ask if he sexually abused you. Your father replied it was because his brother had done it to him, that's what's in the statements.

Your fathers' lawyers said this could be referring to anything from not getting sweeties at the ice cream van to slapping you when you were naughty.

The actual words needed to convict your father never got used, and your father has not admitted to any sexual abuse or any other wrongdoing. The only thing he has confessed to is possibly giving you the odd slap growing up. The fiscal feels there is a lack of evidence against him and said it wouldn't stand up in court. Callum, I am sorry, but your father is a free man, we tried our best, but there is not enough hard evidence to convict him, and in the end, it is only your word against his.

I am devastated by the news, and I can't believe what they are telling me.

After sitting with the police for hours and hours, and going over my statement, reliving the years of hell that beast put me through. It is all for nothing as he has walked free, just like Peg Leg, Karen's father and my uncle Bobby.

I can't understand why the case against my father will not go to court; only due to the way my sister and mother have asked my father what he did to me. I'm confused, and I say to the police, so let me get this right. What you are saying, is that my sister and mother, did not ask my father in specific detail what he did to me, using the word sexual abuse, so he gets to walk free? The police respond to me, yes Callum that is correct, and because yours is a historic case of sexual abuse with no physical evidence to prove what he did.

I say to the police, my mother and sister had just found out what had happened to me when they spoke with my father. My mother's marriage of twenty-eight years was over in a flash, and you expect them to word things right. My mother and sister were sick to their stomachs with what he did to me, and I think it's understandable if they could not bring themselves to say the actual words. It's clear he knew what they were talking about; he even said it was because his brother did it to him, and we all know what that was, his brother was a convicted paedophile. The police say they completely understand my frustration and believe he done this terrible thing; however, in a court of law, there needs to be solid proof. Unfortunately, we don't have the necessary evidence to put him away. You can appeal against this decision and fight it; However, without substantial evidence, you will only be putting yourself and your family through the emotions again. Unless someone other than you came forward, to say that he has sexually abused them or we receive new evidence that can hold up in court, there is nothing more we can do.

When the police leave, I feel hollow inside, it is almost like no one believes me, I'm hurt, and it's sickening, but I'm not about to let my father beat me.

I am now jobless, and soon to be homeless within the next few months, If I don't get off my butt and do something about it. I contact my old work and ask for my job back in the five-star hotel, and after a lengthy interview, I am pleasantly surprised. Not only do I get my old job back, but I also get a promotion to be the deputy in charge of the department.

When I return to work, I ask about all our old work colleagues, and what has happened to them, it was all new faces in our department, and I never knew any of them. I find out most of them moved into the care industry with several new care homes opening in the area. Drake had become a makeup artist and was doing well for himself, and then out of the blue, he committed suicide. I never understood why, as he had so much going for him and was always such a bubbly outgoing guy. The short time that I knew Drake, he impacted my life profoundly, by putting me on the path to finding myself. If Drake never took me to my first gay club, I might still be in the closet and living with my parents.

A few months later, I'm saddened when I meet Daz in town, and he tells me that Rab has also committed suicide. It prompts me to think back to the times I stood on that bridge considering suicide myself; I feel grateful that I did not do it. Now I'm even more determined to live my life.

My house finally sells, and I get more than I expect for it, so due to making a substantial profit from the house sale. I can start fresh, clear all my debts, and move on in life, forgetting about my past with Clay, Karen, and my father. With this extra cash, I have that little boost I need to start my life over.

Over a year has passed since I told my mother about my father, and she is finding it very hard to cope with everything and turns to the alcohol. After much encouragement from family, my mother joins a group to assist with her alcohol abuse and depression.

At her group, my mother meets a larger than life woman called big Sandra. Sandra is a lovely lady, and very straight to the point about things, she knew the story of my father from there group meetings with my mother. Even though she has never met him; she hates him.

Several months have passed since my mother started her group meetings, and I decide to visit her; I want to make sure she is ok and find out how things are going with her sessions.

When I arrive at her house, my mother and big Sandra are sitting in the kitchen. As I enter the kitchen and say hello, big Sandra says to my mother, so Mary, are you going to tell him, or am I? My mother just looked at big Sandra and started mumbling about something completely random, nothing to do with what big Sandra is referring to.

Big Sandra then turns to look directly at me and says, your mother has been meeting up with your father, I've told her it's out of order, and I'm now telling you because I think it's wrong. I'm blown away with what she has said to me and turn to my mother, I ask, is this true? Have you seen him? My mother replies to me, Callum, I needed to get some answers for myself, and I have things I want to know, after all, I was married to him for twenty-eight years.

Big Sandra then pipes up; Mary is that why you kissed him to get your answers, she stood up smiled at me and said, I'm sorry that I was the person to tell you that son, but I think you had the right to know.

I stand there staring at my mother, waiting for an answer and feeling like my soul got ripped out. My mother admits to kissing him and says she is sorry, and that my father is living local about twenty minutes' drive away. I stand there staring at her in disbelief; I am so disgusted; I feel like she must not believe me; how could she if she still wants to talk with him and kiss him.

My mother starts crying and asks, Callum do you want to know something, I wish you never told me. You have destroyed my life, and it's not easy to switch off twenty-eight years of marriage. You can't expect me to just turn off my feelings just like that.

I am infuriated, and without thinking, I throw my mobile phone across the room at her, narrowly missing her face and smashing off the wall. I scream at her how can you do this to me, and give her one final look of disgust, shaking my head at her. Then she starts saying sorry, and telling me she won't talk to him again, and that she never meant what she said. I turn away from her and walk out of her house.

As the month's pass, I discovered I'm not the only person that my father has sexually abused; he has interfered with an older male family member. He had sexually abused him as a child growing up, and when he got too old, my father moved on to me. The other family member never reported sexual abuse; therefore, my father was never charged or questioned for his action.

When I get the opportunity to talk with the family member, I try to convince him to go to the police and give a statement. Explaining how my father also sexually abused me, and he can get prosecuted if we both go forward. This time it will not only be my word against my father's there will be two of us against him.

The family member refuses point-blank to give a statement and tells me they do not want to go through a court case. They have their own family to think about, and it would be too stressful for them and their family. I'm disappointed with him, but I don't pursue the matter. I fully understand the pain it causes when you must go over those horrendous times, as you give your statement to the police. I would not force that on anyone.

Within my family, there are several people you do not cross, and the decision to take care of my father gets made. The family asks my mother and me, are we comfortable with the decision? We both say, yes, so the plan to take care of my father gets put into motion. I don't know the dates, the times or place; I just know it will happen.

A few days after the discussion to take care of my father, I'm in work, and I receive a phone call, when I answered the phone and hear my father's voice at the other end, I go into shock. He says, hello Callum it's your father, I can feel the colour drain from my face, and have this feeling of fear and dread come over me, I instantly look to the window just in case he is outside. I start to stutter at him, why are you calling me at my work? Please don't phone me again.

He answers, Callum, please don't hang up the phone; I just want to ask how you are? I want to say sorry to you personally, and I have sent something to mum's house for you, I still love you, and I will always be your father, and if you need me, I am here for you.

I completely lose control and start screaming at him down the work phone. How dare you fucking call me, and at my work, don't you ever dare call me again, do you hear me? Never call me, I don't want anything to do with you, just fucking leave me alone, and I slam the phone down.

I looked around and realised everyone has stopped what they are doing and staring at me. I put my head in my hands and hide my face, my boss also standing staring at me, says, let's go for a coffee and have a wee chat.

Sitting in the tearoom, I pour my heart out to my boss and say sorry for my behaviour. She is understanding and urges me to contact the police and inform them that my father has phoned my workplace.

The police warn my father and hit him with an injunction; he has to stay away from me and is not permitted to make any form of contact.

A few days after my call at work, a family member came to see me and informed me that the plan to take care of my father has failed. When they arrived at his flat, it was empty; someone had tipped him off, that they were coming for him, and he had packed his stuff and left.

My mother later confessed she had got drunk and went to my father's house, she warned him of the plan to sort him, once and for all and asked him to disappear. My father wasted no time taking her advice; he packed everything went into hiding and changed his name.

Now I have no idea where my father is, or what his new identity is, I'm livid with my mother and the justice system. Because of them, he is out there, and he is entirely free to start doing it all over again, destroying another child's life.

My entire family stop talking with my mother after she met up with my father. She gets given one final ultimatum, that she can choose him or her family, and my sister tells her it's too much of a risk, so she can't see the grandkids. My mother decides her family and grandchildren are more important than my paedophile father, and she agreed never to see or speak with him again.

It takes several weeks for everyone to forgive her; however, I can't so I continue to walk past her in the street, she tries to talk with me, and I just ignore her. It breaks my heart, not talking to my mother, and I want to believe she has stopped meeting my father. However, over the years, my trust has been smashed to bits by everyone I have ever trusted. I must show her that I'm serious, so I continue with my life and exclude my mother from everything I do.

It takes two years before I'm willing to forgive and speak to my mother. Then I see her in the shop, and we say hello to each other. I know she is not keeping well, and she has not spoken with my father since the day I stopped talking to her, so when she invites me to come to her house for a chat, I accept.

Later that night I go to my mothers, and we are talking about many things, the main thing is my father, my mother promises me she has not, and will not speak to him again. As the night goes on, I try to tell my mother in detail what my father did to me; I want her to remember just how evil he is. As we both sit crying, and as I'm opening my heart to her, she asks that I stop, saying she can't listen to anymore as it's just too much for her. I then tell her about him phoning my work and ask, did my father send me anything in the post?

My mother says, yes, he sent a letter to you, it's in that cupboard with all the other paperwork, sorry I forgot all about it.

I say to her I'm hoping it is something I can use as evidence against him.

My mother goes to the cupboard and rummages through the paperwork, she pulls an envelope out and hands it to me. I quickly open the envelope, to find a card filled with money inside, I scan over the contents, I'm looking for anything I can use as evidence. The card reads something like; I'm sorry for not being there on Christmas and your birthday and a whole load of apologies for things, but nothing I can use against him in a court. I take the card and all the money and rip the lot into pieces, and throw it into the bin, I tell my mother I want nothing from my father, and I considered him dead to me. The family also decide to inform all the grandchildren he died before they were born, to prevent any unwanted questions or them wanting to meet with him.

I'm now in my mid-twenties, and things are starting to look up for our family, and we are all supportive of each other. We agree not to let my father come between us or to do more damage than he has already done. We decide from this day and going forward; it is best if we all consider him dead.

A few nights after my father's fake death, my friends take me on a night out, and that's when my life begins to get better, and I meet Ryan. Ryan is tall dark and handsome, with a mysteriousness to him, and I'm drawn to him instantly, with no idea if he is gay or straight. I'm sitting with my friends around the table, and we are all having drinks and a laugh, I'm joking with them and telling them how I find Ryan attractive. I tell them he has been looking over at me, and we have made eye contact a couple of times, and he keeps smiling at me. Then Ryan walks over to my table as he is leaving and passes me his phone number and asks that I call him.

We continually texted each other for two days solid, and then we decide to meet up and go for a hill walk. During our walk, I feel like I have known Ryan for years, we are so comfortable in each other's space, and have so much in common, it's unbelievable. After the hill climb, Ryan walks me home, and we kiss and say goodnight.

For the first time in my life, I'm walking on the clouds and getting butterflies in my stomach, I look to the skies and see all the stars and think of my grandparents, I thank them for sending him to me.

A few weeks pass, and we introduce each other to the families, it's incredible, both our families get on excellent. Ryan has three brothers and two sisters, and I have three brothers and one sister. Our families are so similar to each other it is uncanny, he even has a deaf sibling like me, and I instantly fall in love with him.

Ryans father is the best guy ever, his name is Paddy, and we get on so well, he is everything a true father should be.

On our first anniversary, Ryan and I decide to go on a holiday together, and when on holiday Ryan asks me to marry him. I say yes instantly, and our wedding day gets set for the following year.

The year passes so quickly, and the big day of our wedding has come. We have gone all out and hired several limousines for the family. Made sure there is free-flowing drink at the venue, and the food and decorations are extravagant. Shelby is over the moon to be taking my father's place and giving me away, and Ryan and I have beautiful matching suits. The wedding is a great success, and the hotel room that night is gorgeous and decorated with rose petals and a bottle of champagne. The next morning, we are collected by limousine and taken to the air-port, where we fly off to the med for our honeymoon.

We are a match made in heaven, and I can't believe my luck, with each year that passes, our relationship grows stronger.

Ryans father, Paddy and I are talking one day in his kitchen, and he asked if I liked camping and fishing and the likes. I tell him I have never done anything like that, as my father was not that kind of guy. Paddy asks, what kind of guy was your father, what did he do?

I tell Paddy, growing up we never did any activities with our parents, my father was never kind to my family or me. He abused my mother and us as children, and he has moved away, we consider him dead, and we don't talk about him.

It's during my time with Paddy that I discover, how a father should be with his child. Paddy decided over the next few years; he will do all the things with me; he did with his children and grandchildren. He takes me to visit all the best spots, and we have fantastic times together with all his family. Paddy takes me fishing over at the shore, and we collect Wilkes and Muscles and have such a great time. We have big family barbecues and go camping, we visit so many places, he teaches me to build camp-fires, and we all sit around the fire with a guitar and sing songs. Paddy even knows about all the stars in the sky, and he chats with me about all the constellations; he is fantastic and very kind to me.

Thanks to Paddy I don't miss out on my childhood, I just have mine later than most. I'm so grateful for the time Ryans' father shares with me. Unfortunately, he dies suddenly, and both Ryan and I are devastated. Paddy was the glue of our family and always brought everyone together; he gave me twelve of the best years of my life, and I loved him like a real father.

I'm now in my early thirties, and I still have nightmares about my father. I wake Ryan up regularly during the night, shouting in my sleep, and gasping for air. I have this reoccurring dream that my father has sneaked into my room at night and is suffocating me with a pillow. I don't think what my father did will ever leave me; however, as the year's pass, I learn to cope with what happened to me, and I refuse to let him beat me.

My mother begins to have difficulty breathing, and after a visit to the hospital, we discover she has cancer. She is so upset and scared, so our family all pool together and support her.

After lots of tests and visits to the hospital, they operate on her and remove several tumours, lymph nodes and half of her left lung. Then after the operation, she gets chemotherapy to kill any cancer leftover. During her chemotherapy, my mother starts to lose her hair, so being positive about it, she requests all the family go to her house for a big party. At the party, she asks my brother to do the honours and remove the remainder of her hair. It is so emotional as he shaves her head and very upsetting, yet at the same time, bonding for our family. The party makes us all realise the importance of family, and how my father has just been a tiny pinprick in our lives.

THE FINAL CHAPTER

Now in my late thirties, my mother and I are very close, we talk openly about things and regret the times that we fell out over my father. The doctors recently discovered two new tumours in my mother's right lung, and they say they will not operate as it will cause more harm. I realise time now is very precious with my mother, and I resent my father for the years he stole away from us. I blame him for her going into that psychiatric hospital, and for the two years we had fallen out, as I will never get that time back.

When my father's side of the family discovered what he did to me, it caused a rift. However, I still wish them well on birthdays and Christmas through social media. My Aunt Carol and Jane are still living in England and now have grandkids. My uncle Josh became a millionaire, he retired abroad, and he still has no grandchildren. As for evil uncle Bobby, I'm not sure if he is alive or dead, my preference would be that he died, and my Grandpa Word lived a very long life and died at one hundred years old.

I still have no contact with Karen after what she did to me, and I tried to find out what happened to old Jack and his little Jack Russel. Some say he died, and others say he moved away, whatever happened with Jack, I hope he had some good years.

Thirty years after my first gay kiss, I bumped into Ian at the bank; it was one of those awkward moments and can't avoid it. I said hello, and we spoke briefly, then he made a point of telling me he was happily married with two kids, so I guess he wasn't gay after all.

Shelby and I are still best of friends after twenty-odd years, we don't see each other as often as I would like, but we have an unbreakable friendship bond.

My sister is still as strong as ever, marching through life and helping others; she cares for my disabled brother, looks after our mother, and now also helps out with a grandchild of her own. My sister has been and continues to be the most reliable support in my life. My father never sexually abused any of my brothers, which relieved my guilt for leaving them in that house with him, and brothers have all grown to be fine young men with good jobs.

Many times, Senga and my mother asked me to chat with a counsellor about my father; they said it would help me. I could never bring myself to speak with a counsellor, so Senga then told me to write my feelings down on paper. I decided to take her advice and started writing, and as I write, I feel the burden of my father lift from me; It's been emotional.

I make a promise to myself that I will never treat anyone as my father treated me, nor will I let it happen to another. I also wanted to change my career to help others, so I change my job and become a support worker in a challenging behaviour unit. The Unit is for adults with learning difficulties and Autism. I love my job, and every day it reminds me to be grateful for what I have, and never to take it for granted.

In my spare time, I have a YouTube channel, and I run my own Airbnb business, and now I have written this book.

It is April 2020, and I will turn forty this month, and It scares me to think that my father is still out there somewhere with his new identity. I only pray that he stopped; however, it is unlikely.

Thank you for taking the time to read my life story.

Kindest Regards

C.S Proctor

Note to my father

Dear dad

If you ever get the opportunity to read my book, you were wrong, I did amount to something, and I did it all without you.

I hope your guilt eats away at you, and my forgiveness awaits your confession.

CONFIDENTIAL HELP

If you or someone you know has experienced or is still experiencing sexual abuse. Please speak out, as I wish I had spoken out the first time it happened to me. The person who is abusing you can and will get stopped, and they will never hurt you again. The helplines are completely private and confidential, and you don't even need to give a name. Please call even if it's just to chat, there were so many times I could have taken my own life, so please don't be afraid to ask for the help; it is out there.

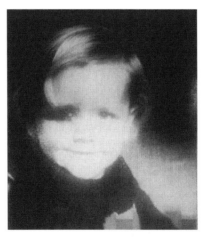

This book tells the true story of a family's pain as several harrowing events unfold. A grandmother so selfish she lost everything over one man's sick pleasure. A dark evil secret forced between a father and son. The loving mother so broke down in life she questions her sanity. A child's cries that no one heard, with beatings that no one stopped. The teachers who got it all wrong. A lifelong friendship scorned, and the beast that caused it all.

Printed in Great Britain
by Amazon